Dear 7ᵗʰ Path Student,

As the first 7ᵗʰ Path practitioner, I would like to welcome you to The Path! You have just begun a new and transforming personal process of Mind-Body-And-Spirit.

To protect the 7ᵗʰ Path Recognitions, we require that all students sign this form before learning 7ᵗʰ Path Self-Hypnosis®. By signing this form, you promise that you will not teach these Recognitions to anyone else unless you become a Certified 7ᵗʰ Path™ Teacher. The Recognitions are copyrighted and the term 7ᵗʰ Path Self-Hypnosis® is a registered trademark.

Once again, Welcome to The Path™!

Calvin D. Banyan
The First 7ᵗʰ Path™ Practitioner

Please print or write clearly:

Your Name: _____

Address:_____

_____

Email: _____

Your Signature: _____

Your 7ᵗʰ Path Teacher's Name: _____

Date: _____

Where you learned the 7ᵗʰ Path™ (City, State, Country, etc.):

_____

Please complete this form and hand it back to your 7ᵗʰ Path teacher before you learn 7ᵗʰ Path.

(We do not sell or share this information with anyone.)

Get On the Path and Program Yourself for Success
Study Guide for 7th Path Self-Hypnosis®
(2nd Edition)
By Calvin D. Banyan

Banyan Hypnosis Center for Training & Services, Inc.
To contact us, go to: www.7thPathSelfHypnosis.com

Second Edition

Recognition of Gratitude

My gratitude goes out to Marc Drucker, Tracy Holwagner, Susan Just, Bonnie LeClair, Kelsey Banyan, and Maureen Banyan for their assistance in editing this book. Also, I'm grateful to John Paul Rawlins who helped in the cover redesign for this 2nd Edition.

Contents

Chapter 1
Welcome to the Path

This is a guide to using the 7th Path Self-Hypnosis® system. It is meant to accompany the work that you are doing with a 7th Path Self-Hypnosis® Teacher, with your hypnotist, or it can be used as an approach to personal change on your own, working with a recorded version of the class available on compact discs (CDs).

This booklet was written so that everyone introduced to the 7th Path Self-Hypnosis® system will receive at least this minimum amount of information about this holistic form of self-hypnosis. Many times, in class or in hypnosis sessions, there simply is not enough time to cover all of the helpful bits and nuances about this system. *Get on the Path* is a brief explanation to help you understand and use 7th Path Self-Hypnosis® (also referred to as 7th Path™ in this book).

You may notice that there is a certain amount of repetition in this book. Repetition is the mother of learning. Repetition is used to emphasize important points and to make it easier to learn the material.

Note: If your copy of this booklet is a photocopy, then it may be out of date and illegal. Photocopies are not authorized. If you have received a photocopy of this book please contact us at (800) 965-3390 or (469) 969-2176.

Do not attempt to teach the 7th Path Self-Hypnosis® System without proper training

By receiving this information, you agree not to teach it to anyone else unless you have been trained as a 7th Path Self-Hypnosis® Teacher. You will be taught this process in a very specific manner. The process of learning and teaching 7th Path Self-Hypnosis® involves the use of hypnotism. If the use of hypnosis is not employed in the teaching of 7th Path™, then the process is not being followed, and it can greatly diminish the power of the self-hypnosis and Recognitions. This will be discussed further in the section on "How do I get more Recognitions?"

If you do not agree with the above paragraph, please return this book to your teacher or hypnotist, and let him or her know about your decision not to learn this process of self-hypnosis.

What is 7th Path Self-Hypnosis®?

The 7th Path Self-Hypnosis® system consists of a series of hypnotic suggestions and a special technique for using them that will result in positive personal change. It is unlike any other system of self-hypnosis that came before it. It is different because it has built-in steps that work toward removing old subconscious barriers to successful living *before* you give yourself any self-hypnosis suggestions for the changes that you want to make.

Some aspects of the process are like an anti-virus program that computer owners use to remove destructive programs from their computers. This "program" will work to remove the little limiting programs that you have picked up over your lifetime (i.e., bad habits and erroneous beliefs in limitation and the painful emotions that they generate). You will learn to use this system to literally reprogram yourself for success.

Good things will happen while you are removing the old programming. Because the subconscious and conscious levels of your mind know why you are using this process of self-hypnosis (i.e. increase motivation, improve self-esteem, etc.), it is common to start experiencing some positive changes before any suggestions are ever directly given for the specific changes that you want to make. For example, you might have come to learn 7th Path™ because you want to work on weight loss, stress reduction, or sports improvement. Using the 7th Path™ system, you will not give yourself hypnotic suggestions *directed* at the changes you want to make on your particular issue until you receive the 5th Recognition. However, it is often reported by practitioners of this system that they quickly make substantial progress toward their goals, such as losing weight, or feeling a reduction of stress, or improvement in your sport, etc., while still in the process of removing old programming.

After you have begun using 7th Path Self-Hypnosis®, if at any time you want to move ahead more quickly, or if you ever feel "stuck," talk to your hypnotherapist or teacher. You may benefit from receiving a few private sessions. Individual sessions like these can greatly improve your progress through the use of hypnotherapy, or by discovering and correcting any problems that you may be experiencing in your application of this process (due to misunderstanding how to do the process). We recommend that you choose a 5-PATH® Certified Hypnotherapist to work with if you choose to work with a hypnotherapist while using this process.

The 7th Path Self-Hypnosis® system is designed to remove the old programming that is preventing you from being successful. Removing old barriers is accomplished by using the first four Recognitions of the 7th Path Self-Hypnosis® system. This work will be taught while you are in class (live or recorded) or during your hypnosis sessions with your hypnotherapist, if you are working with one.

If you are using the 7th Path Self-Hypnosis® system and not working with anyone else such as a 7th Path™ Teacher that is perfectly alright. If you have questions, you may contact our office and find out if there is such a person near you. We also encourage you to join our online community of 7th Path Self-Hypnosis® practitioners, where you can get your questions answered online or share your experiences. Visit our web site or call our office for the latest information about our online support.

Where did the 7th Path Self-Hypnosis® system come from?

The 7th Path Self-Hypnosis® system was developed as a result of thousands of hours of therapy work with clients in hypnosis. Through careful observation of our many clients who were making the positive changes that they came in to make, it was noted what kind of insights commonly led to success. Also, 7th Path™ was influenced by pure inspiration and experience with other systems of self-improvement and psychological training.

The 7th Path™ system is a form of self-hypnosis. One of the few mistakes that some of our clients make when learning to use the techniques of the 7th Path Self-Hypnosis® system is to attempt to turn it into some other technique that they have used in the past (i.e. meditation or visualization). It differs in that it is not *necessarily* a form of religious or philosophical practice; *it is directed at overcoming normal everyday issues that affect many people,* and it is much easier to do than the vast majority of meditation techniques available.

Furthermore, in meditation, it is often the intent of the practitioner to focus only on one thought or idea throughout the period of meditation. This is *not* the case when using the 7th Path Self-Hypnosis® system. This major difference makes the 7th Path™ practice much easier to do than meditation. If your mind wanders for a bit, that is okay: 7th Path™ is a very forgiving practice. Having other thoughts is *not only okay, it is useful! You are supposed to have other thoughts!* This will be expanded on later as I explain the actual practice.

Chapter 2
Hypnosis and Self-Hypnosis

Since the 7th Path™ system is a form of self-hypnosis, I find it helpful to spend some time discussing hypnosis. There are many misconceptions about hypnosis; for right now, let's just think of hypnosis as focused attention, like when you are driving and you forget to make that turn on the freeway, or when you are so immersed in a television show that you don't notice when someone is talking to you. Hypnosis is a perfectly natural state of mind that all human beings experience thousands of times during their lives.

The United States Dictionary of Occupational Titles defines hypnosis as "acceptable selective thinking" and "bypass of the critical factor." The definition can use a little more explanation. "Acceptable selective thinking," means that you are choosing to selectively attend to something; like if your mind wanders, you take your attention back to what you intend to focus upon. For example, a hypnotherapist, hypnotist, or your 7th Path™ Teacher, may have you keep your attention on a series of instructions to help you relax your body while learning to do this process. This is what is meant by "selective thinking." Of course, at any time you could decide to no longer attend to the relaxation process, and then you would begin to emerge from hypnosis.

The next part of the definition is "the bypass of the critical factor," meaning that the critical part of your thinking is suspended temporarily. From my experience, I have come to understand the critical factor as a kind of comparing mechanism of the mind. Whenever new information is suggested, the mind compares that information with what it already "knows" on the subject or topic. If the new information is too different from what you "know" (or believe) about the subject, the new information is rejected (and filed away). If it is similar to what the individual already "knows" about the world, it is easily filed away into the subconscious mind where your beliefs reside. Once that information has been accepted, it becomes a part of you, and you will tend to use that information subconsciously and automatically.

When someone is in hypnosis and either giving herself suggestions or receiving them from someone else (i.e., a hypnotist) , the suggestion is accepted, and any conflicting information is replaced, as long as the individual in the hypnotic state feels that accepting the suggestion is in his or her best interest. This is the power of hypnosis. It can be a very powerful and important tool for helping people make good positive changes in their lives. By learning 7th Path Self-Hypnosis® you will have this power available for the rest of your life.

If you have any further questions about hypnosis, please feel free to talk to your 7th Path™ Teacher. He or she will be happy to answer any questions that you have about hypnosis, hypnotherapy or the 7th Path Self-Hypnosis® system. Additional information is also available on our web sites at *www.HypnosisCenter.com* and *www.7thPathSelfHypnosis.com*.

Chapter 3
The 7th Path Holistic Self-Hypnosis System

Who benefits by using the 7th Path Self-Hypnosis® system?

"Give a man a fish and you feed him for a day. Teach him how to fish and you feed him for life," summarizes the primary intent of the 7th Path Self-Hypnosis® system. Once you have learned how to use the 7th Path Self-Hypnosis® system, you can keep yourself free from erroneous programming in the future, and use self-hypnosis to help you reach almost any goal that you care to achieve in the future.

7th Path Self-Hypnosis® is a mind-body-spirit approach, and works best for those who believe in some kind of higher power, *but any such belief in a "Higher Power" is not required in order to use the Basic Recognitions.* This will be discussed in more detail shortly, but let it suffice for now to say that a spiritual approach is not necessary for successful use of the 7th Path Self-Hypnosis® system. One can simply focus on natural concepts rather than the spiritual and it still works very well. This is especially true for the first five Recognitions. Moving beyond the first five Recognitions almost requires a spiritual belief system of some kind, but it has been shown through practice that if someone *really wanted* to use all the steps and do it without any kind of spiritual concept, she could do so. This will become clear as you begin using the system.

I belabor the point because I want to be very sensitive to the rights and concerns of anyone who might come in contact with the system. It is possible to misunderstand what is going on here and think that the 7th Path Self-Hypnosis® system is some kind of religion in and of itself. It is not. Rather, it is a way of integrating *your* particular religious or spiritual beliefs into this process of self-improvement. It is meant to be complementary to the beliefs that you already hold. It is a way to use your highest beliefs and bring them more actively into your everyday life. This process has been used by members of every great religion of the world as well as agnostics and atheists.

Why bring spirituality into this at all?

At our center, we like to promote the use of a mind-body-spirit approach whenever it is acceptable to our clients. *This is because using such high concepts and beliefs seem to promote a faster, more powerful, and more permanent change.* We do not promote or discourage any particular belief system. The individuals who are a part of our organization themselves come from a variety of beliefs, and we respect them all.

Your hypnotherapist or 7th Path™ Teacher is very thoughtful and understanding in this area. She is trained to work with you, whether you want to use a spiritual approach or not. She should be able to work with you and whatever belief system you have, even if you prefer not to reveal what that is. Practitioners of the 7th Path Self-Hypnosis® system should feel very comfortable using the 7th Path™ system no matter what religious background he or she comes from (even none at all).

All that being said, the 7th Path Self-Hypnosis® system can be a very spiritual practice, *if that is your intent.* In addition to being a very powerful system of personal change, some who have learned the 7th Path Self-Hypnosis® system have taken it to another level and used it in groups, where the different practitioners get together and do it as a group practice. This kind of group practice reportedly feels very supportive in nature. Some things are just nice to do together and 7th Path™ practice seems to be one of them. If you enjoy working together in groups, then this approach may be just what you wanted. On the other hand, if you prefer to practice in private, that is also a wonderful way to experience 7th Path™.

Some practitioners have even adopted 7th Path™ as a devotional practice (e.g., clergy, nuns, and laypersons). In this form, people from all over the world, from any of the major religious or spiritual backgrounds, can gather together and do this. Again, this is neither encouraged or discouraged, nor is it required; it is mentioned here for your personal information.

What can the 7th Path Self-Hypnosis® system do for me?

It is impossible to guarantee results. Everyone is so different, and your intent is very important in determining the kind of results that you will experience. At this time (because we simply have not had sufficient experience in this area), *we are not recommending the use of the 7th Path Self-Hypnosis® system for anyone who has a serious mental illness.* If you have received such a diagnosis, then you should only do this practice under the supervision of your attending physician or mental health professional, such as a psychologist or counselor. Due to the powerful and emotional nature of this practice, individuals with such mental illnesses may not benefit from the practice and may even experience an increase in their symptoms. Examples of serious mental illnesses include, but not limited to: Major Depression, Schizophrenia, and Borderline Personality Disorder.

The 7th Path Self-Hypnosis® system was designed for normal everyday people with normal everyday problems and goals. If you fit into this category, as most of us do, I think you will be very pleased with your results.

The 7th Path Self-Hypnosis® system sets you free from old patterns that have limited you up to this point in almost any area of your life. It also lets you choose what kind of new patterns and beliefs you would like to establish and reinforce for ongoing personal improvement and change.

It can also provide you with new spiritual direction in your life and a feeling of connection to your higher power. (I will no longer discuss how spirituality is *not* required but helpful; I think that I have said enough about that.)

Removal of internal stress is part of the program

An effect that seems to be associated with regular use of this system is a feeling of calm, often described as feeling more relaxed, patient and peaceful, or in control. As stress is removed from your body and subconscious mind, which is there in the form of old useless emotions, there is a tendency toward health and optimism. How stress affects your health will be discussed at greater detail in a later chapter.

As stress is removed from your body and nervous system, some physical changes, both temporary and permanent may occur. Temporary physical experiences may include a jerking of an arm or leg while doing hypnosis (like when you are going to sleep at night). You may notice a temporary change in your digestive tract and elimination processes. Even temporary rashes have been reported. The key word here is "temporary." Your body and nervous system are adjusting to a healthier state. Some people will experience detoxification symptoms. If you do, we recommend that you drink more water.

Permanent changes may include loss of a pattern of headaches, muscle pain, or joint pain. Symptoms associated with stress induced illness are usually greatly reduced or completely eliminated. We cannot say that these things will happen, just that they have been reported by many of the practitioners. *7th Path™ is not intended or recommended as an alternative to any medical process, procedure, or program, but may be used as a complement to any medical condition where stress reduction may improve your condition.* Consult with your physician if you want to use 7th Path™ to complement any medical intervention. We will be happy to work with your physician. Other physicians have reported benefits of using 7th Path™ along with a medical approach.

Hypnosis and self-hypnosis, in and of itself, does not heal anything. Rather, in many cases when healing does occur, it is as a result of the reduction of stress that the practitioner was holding inside herself, and which was released during the 7th Path Self-Hypnosis® process. As a result of this elimination of stress, the body has healed itself.

Chapter 4
Getting Started On the 7th Path

First, before you learn or practice any of the techniques associated with the 7th Path Self-Hypnosis® system, I want to give you a gentle warning. This is a very powerful system. The techniques are designed to remove old emotions that may have gotten in the way of your success (such as anger, guilt, and fear). Most often, when practicing 7th Path™, you will feel very relaxed and comfortable, but sometimes you may feel antsy, or otherwise uncomfortable. *Feeling emotional is sometimes part of this process. When this happens, feel optimistic; you are doing good work and the process is working.* Once the feeling has been fully experienced, it is doubtful that you will have to experience it again - it will probably have been released. If it is experienced in subsequent sessions, it will probably be less intense and eventually fade away to nothing.

Some practitioners may experience these symptoms (experiencing emotions such as anger) in between their self-hypnosis sessions. This especially occurs while working on the 2nd and 3rd Recognitions. This will usually pass when you begin the 4th Recognition. Also, using the Recognitions as autosuggestions (saying them to yourself in the normal waking state) can reduce this experience. Again, it is temporary; it is part of the reprogramming at work. We call this process the "emptying of the cup."

What is a Recognition and how do they work?

A "Recognition" is a positive self-statement that resonates throughout your nervous system. Because the mind works by association, it will "resonate" with similar thoughts and beliefs that you have. It will also "bump" up against beliefs that are in opposition to the positive suggestion. The process will reinforce positive thoughts and beliefs. It may also have a tendency to make your regular thoughts more positive throughout the day. Also, the recognition will work toward, cancel out, or weaken your negative thoughts and limiting beliefs that generate the associated painful emotions.

The Recognitions work like little heat-seeking missiles. Through the process of resonance they seek out, find, weaken and ultimately remove old programs that get in the way of success in life, such as a reoccurring thought or feeling that "I'm not good enough." They reinforce good programs that generate positive thoughts and behaviors. *Remember, what you are thinking has a direct affect on what you do in life and how you feel. Thinking and feeling more positively may also attract more positive people, events and opportunities into your life.*

Feelings result from perceptions about the world (as we have come to expect and believe it to be), and the thoughts that you have about those perceptions. Emotional forces are among the most motivating factors in your life. Over time, emotions tend to win out over willpower. So if you have been using willpower alone in an attempt to make positive changes in your life and you have had only limited success, changing how you feel inside may be just what you have been looking for. That is exactly what this system will do for you.

Chapter 5
Emotions and Freeing Yourself from Old Programming

Feelings and emotions come from three different places: your past, present, and future. How you are feeling at any given moment is a result of your thoughts, perceptions, and beliefs about your past and present situations, in addition to how you expect your future to be. These thoughts and the resulting beliefs built up over your entire lifetime.

Probably most of your thoughts and beliefs are right on the mark and are an accurate representation of reality. This is especially true of the beliefs that you are consciously aware of holding. But we also have subconscious beliefs. Some of these may not be so correct (perhaps because they were formed in childhood when you were not as well informed as you are now about the world.) Gosh, it would be nice to have known then what you know now—as an adult. Fortunately, it is never too late to change those old core beliefs and the emotions that they generate, such as fear, anger and guilt.

Have you ever had the experience of *thinking* one thing is true but *feeling* differently about it? Let me explain what I mean. Most people, if asked about the kind of person they are, would say that they are a good person and smart enough to handle their lives quite well. Yet sometimes, in some situations, even though they might *think* they are up to the situation at hand, they may not *feel* that way.

Please let me go on about this a little more. For example, you might enroll in a speech class. You know consciously that you can handle the class or you would not have signed up for it. But when it comes time for that first speech you might become uneasy or even frightened. The protective part of you (which lives in the subconscious mind) is generating thoughts like "what the heck am I doing here?!" Your subconscious mind shouts from deep within you, "I have got to get out of here, or I will make a fool of myself!" The subconscious mind is trying to protect you. If this kind of thing has happened to you, then in your history you have probably been embarrassed by public speaking. The intent of the subconscious mind is good, the outcome is not because it can limit your ability to move on and grow.

When you experience this internal conflict, what we have is a definite difference of opinion! You started off *thinking* that you could do something, but when it came right down to it, you *felt* like you could not handle the situation.

Unless some reprogramming of the subconscious mind occurs, you may always feel like running away from opportunities that involve public speaking. In fact, if you let it go on, your situation can become worse. If you avoid these anxiety provoking situations, it becomes a habit. By avoiding the thing or situation that you fear, you reinforce it in your nervous system causing the fear to become even more powerful!

"Seething Cauldron of Emotions:" a model for understanding how you feel

There is another way to think about this whole thing; I like to use the example of "The Seething Cauldron of Emotions." Take a look at the graphic below. I will use it to explain how your past, present and future can all cause stress in your life. If you don't take into account these three different sources of stress, any attempt at taking back control of how you feel will be inadequate in the long run.

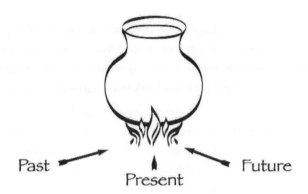

The "cauldron" and that which may be seething inside of it represents your emotional state at any given moment. In this graphic example, you can see that underneath the cauldron is a small flame, and that the flame is fed by three different fuel sources: the past, the present, and the future. Right now, how relaxed, calm or even anxious you feel depends on these three factors. These three factors, in time, come into play in every situation in your life; your past, the present, and your expectations about your future affect you every minute of your life.

In order to feel perfectly calm and peaceful, three things have to be in place. First, you have to be in a place right now in which you perceive to be safe and secure. Next, you must have removed any emotions from the past such as fear, anger or guilt. Finally, you must perceive that your future is also a place of safety.

If you are carrying painful feelings from the past inside you, subconsciously you will be unable to feel safe, perfectly calm and peaceful now. You may attempt to distract yourself from the feelings by engaging in pleasant activities such as eating your favorite foods, or you might attempt to sedate yourself through the use of alcohol or other drugs; but the cause of the feeling remains inside of you, simmering away.

To learn more about how stress can lead to alcohol and/or drug abuse, overeating and bad habits, as well as how to you can eliminate these problems, I recommend reading my book, *The Secret Language of Feelings*. It makes for a wonderful companion piece to what you will be doing with 7th Path Self-Hypnosis®; ask your hypnotherapist or 7th Path Self-Hypnosis® Teacher about it, and they can usually provide you with a copy that you can purchase. You can also go to *www.TheSecretLanguageofFeelings.com* and learn more about it there, and purchase a copy.

Back to the Seething Cauldron of Emotions, if you expect something painful to occur in the future (such as criticism or failure), you will experience a future-oriented fear called worry. Even though you may now be hundreds of miles away from any future pain, the nagging worry will exist either consciously or subconsciously. Clearly, in order to experience a state of perfect calm and peacefulness, we need to be aware of how we are experiencing our past and future.

Realistically for most of us, attempting to reach a state of perfect calm and peacefulness, "in the now," or present would seem impossible. Fortunately, achieving this kind of peace and calmness is not required in order to accomplish whatever you came to the 7th Path Self-Hypnosis® system to do. (Just as a note, many 7th Path™ Practitioners have reported reaching levels of calm and peacefulness that they had never before imagined as a result of using this system.)

Obtaining such a state of ultimate calm would be a wonderful and healthy experience, and you may be surprised at how close you can come to it after practicing for a while. It could be an ultimate goal. However, for most of us, if we could just go from our "normal" state of chronic anxiety and stress to something that approaches a state of perfect calm and peacefulness, we could benefit tremendously! Long before we approach this kind of emotional balance, we can benefit greatly. Here is why: again we will use the "cauldron" as a model.

In the cauldron example, the "past", the "now," and the "future" all contribute to how warm or hot it is. Examples of emotions from the past that can contribute to the heat are fear, guilt and anger. *Fear* is an example of an emotion that can be generated in the present. *Worry* is the perfect example of an emotion that can be generated by your thoughts and perceptions regarding your expectations about the future.

Let's continue with the example of the fear of public speaking. I've worked with a lot of people who have a terrible fear of speaking to groups of any size! The fear can become overwhelming—way out of proportion to the situation.

Here is what is going on:

- You experienced embarrassment speaking before a group in your past.

- Through the process of resonance you continue to experience fear in similar situations.

- You find out that you need to speak before a group again at some point in the future.

- The embarrassment you experienced in the past is expected to occur in a future event.

- Even though you are not in the situation yet, you are experiencing anxiety over an event that has not happened yet, so you feel it now, or anytime in your present when you think about the upcoming event.

- When you are in the situation, emotional resonance brings back the scary feeling from the past.

- When the dreaded event arrives, because of the fear, you do poorly, reinforcing the fear response.

- If you avoid or flee the situation, avoidance or fleeing (behavior) is reinforced because it kept you from experiencing the fear or expected embarrassment. You are caught in a cycle, a self-defeating program.

Even if there was no real danger of being embarrassed, you end up feeling the fear or anxiety about it anyway, despite any conscious effort on your part to calm yourself.

Your fears about the future are coming from your expectations regarding the future and your history concerning similar situations in the past. To reduce the anxiety, we need to neutralize the pattern created in your past or it will continue to bring up the fear every time you find yourself in a similar situation or it can even become worse.

The 7th Path™ System of self-hypnosis uses this same principle of resonance, specifically "emotional resonance" to dissolve this old programming. This is a big part of how the 7th Path Self-Hypnosis® system works. The Recognitions go in and find irrational fears and beliefs and neutralizes them. You can become free of all that baggage which you have been carrying around. Feelings held inside of you that have resulted from your life experience, such as anger, guilt, fear, frustration and depression can all be neutralized through this simple process of self-hypnosis.

How do I use these Recognitions?

You will learn how to take yourself into hypnosis and give yourself suggestions for clearing out the old to make room for the new. We often refer to this part of the 7th Path Self-Hypnosis® system as "the cup emptying phase."

Most of us, by the time we reach about 16 years of age, have pretty much made up our minds about how the world works and have established an identity. This identity includes all of our beliefs about ourselves, including what we believe ourselves to be capable of or incapable of. Our capabilities include our skills and talents. Beliefs about being incapable include all of our limiting beliefs and other judgments that we have made about ourselves, or judgments that others have made about us and that we have accepted without question. For example, some of us are old enough to have been programmed to believe that women are only capable of being mothers, or doing some other motherly-like jobs, perhaps working as cooks, maids, nurses or seamstresses. These limiting beliefs are merely products of an individual's environment and social conditioning. They certainly are not the beliefs that people growing up today in the USA or other highly developed countries are accepting as true.

After the removal of these limiting programs, any good healthy programs that you have will be able to begin to start functioning without the hindrance of false limitations. It is because of this that practitioners of the 7th Path™ system often experience the changes they want to make before they actually start giving themselves suggestions for change. For example, we are programmed genetically to eat just the right amount to remain healthy. But somewhere along the line, new erroneous programming can be accepted that would cause you to become overweight.

Once the erroneous programming has been removed (such as you must clean your plate before you leave the table), your natural God or Nature-given programming can begin to run again and you will begin to become slim and healthy. I believe this is also true for behaviors such as smoking, alcohol abuse, etc. Once the programming that has been installed by marketing and society has been removed, these problems will either spontaneously end, or will be much easier to end with less effort than before. You will then be on your way to a much happier, healthier and successful life.

These problematic programs often have a high degree of emotion attached to them. That is one reason why they are so resistant to change using willpower alone, self-help programs, or even talk therapies. Talking about problems or learning new information only works with the conscious mind. By working exclusively with the conscious mind in those ways, one can rarely overcome the power of emotionally motivated programs in the long run.

Getting free of these old emotionally laden programs, such as being shy because of a belief in inadequacy or fear of criticism, removes a great deal of stress from your body. This is an insidious kind of stress because you become accustomed to it; you begin to feel that it is normal. It is amazing what we can become accustomed to! As shown in the cauldron example, all of those emotions from the past can just sit there inside us, stressing our nervous system and using up our energy. This can eventually lead to physical and mental illness – stress has been linked to hypertension, ulcers, headaches and etc. Furthermore, most medical professionals will tell you that stress will make almost any illness worse.

A stressed-out individual is a breeding ground for psychogenic illnesses. The body of a stressed-out individual is much less equipped to heal itself than a person who is in a state of peace, relaxation or calm. This chronic stress can produce chemical imbalances in your body that can lead to gaining weight and a host of other problems. This is yet another reason why this system complements medical treatments directed at the healing of almost any kind of chronic illness.

I'd like you to think about your genes for a moment. Under a microscope of sufficient power, you would see that they are arranged into something that could be described as looking like a chain. In the illustration below I have drawn a chain.

Let the chain in the illustration represent your genetic code for a moment. Imagine that each link in the chain represents a major organ, function or feature of your body. Every chain has its weakest link, and so does every body. Some people have strong bones. Some of us have great teeth, relative to others that we know. We also have physical weaknesses that are relative to our physical strengths. For example, you may have great skin, but a weak stomach.

And so it goes. Each genetic code has its weaknesses. It is these weaknesses that are most vulnerable under stress, like the chain whose weakest link begins to give when a powerful load is applied to it. It is the weakest link that gives first, then the second, and so on.

Powerful Load  *Powerful Load*

This happens with people too. Under pressure individuals will respond differently. Some will develop ulcers, others will lose their hair, and others will experience hives, and so on. Under chronic stress, the symptoms and disease can be even worse. Stress can lead or contribute to heart attack, stroke, cancer, and much more.

Internal Stress  *External Stress*

In this example there are two kinds of stress, **Internal Stress** and **External Stress**. The kind of stress illustrated by the arrow pointing to the left above is **Internal Stress**. This is the stress caused by the emotional pressure inside us, often coming from unresolved or insufficiently addressed feelings from the past. 7th Path™ will go to work on these stressors right away.

The arrow on the right represents **External Stress**, such as work, school, family and all of the things that can cause us to feel any kind of emotional pain, such as worry, guilt, anger, etc. Much of this is made worse through a process I call emotional resonance. By emotional resonance, I mean that situations in the present can cause us to experience emotions from the past (i.e., the overreaction to situations that we sometimes experience). Since the energy that causes us to overreact to external stress also comes from our past (as shown in the cauldron illustration), when we reduce or eliminate the emotions stored up from the past we automatically reduce our experience of stress caused by external factors.

Looking at it this way, we can see how removing the stress from the past (painful emotions) can create a much healthier body to live in. Your body becomes better able to heal and maintain itself. But it is much better than that!

All of that internal stress that you have been holding onto inside of you is made out of your energy! Once it has been properly removed, you no longer need to use up your energy to maintain those painful emotions.

You also get to benefit in another way. An equal or greater amount of your energy has been used to suppress those feelings. You stuffed them back somehow so that you could continue to function without being bothered by them. When you get rid of the internal stress, you also get back the energy that you have been using to keep them under control.

That is right. How could you get any of your work done or be a parent and all of that if you let those feelings come up all the time? No one would want to be around you! So you suppress them. How do you do that? You put a lid on them and that lid is also made out of your energy! To hold all of that down, it took an equal or greater amount of energy! Once you have removed all of those painful feelings of the past, you get all of that energy back to do what you want to with it. You also get back the energy that you were burning up 24 hours a day, 7 days a week, to suppress those painful emotions from your past. Done properly, with the 7th Path™ system, you can bring a very abundant source of energy into your life and it can start happening very quickly. Most people report having more energy and feeling healthier in just a couple of days.

Now, you can begin to understand how you can really benefit from this practice of self-hypnosis before you ever give yourself suggestions for a specific change.

The 5th Recognition is designed to give yourself suggestions for the specific changes that you want to make. These suggestions will be able to work better than if you did not take the time to undo the old programming, using Recognitions One through Four (I'm repeating myself, I know).

How will I receive these Recognitions?

You will learn the exact wording of the 1st Recognition while in the usual conscious state of mind without being hypnotized. It is given in the pages that follow. It will be used to describe to you how to use the techniques. Then the Recognitions will be given to you while in hypnosis. From then on, the Recognitions are provided to you in the hypnotic state. "Why" you ask?

It is simply more effective to teach you the rest of the Recognitions in hypnosis. In the hypnotic state, we bypass the usual filtering mechanism of the conscious mind known as the critical factor or critical function. The suggestion is then more readily accepted and starts working more quickly and more powerfully. When the Recognitions are received in the hypnotic state they can be called hypnotic suggestions.

Also, while you are in hypnosis, it will be suggested that whenever you want to re-enter the hypnotic state, all you have to do is start repeating the 1st Recognition to yourself and that process will re-induce hypnosis (providing that you intend it to do so and that you are in a safe and comfortable place). You will always be able to emerge from hypnosis whenever you want.

The Recognitions can be used in two general ways. The first is just as I was describing above. Take some time and set it aside to do the process with your eyes closed and deeply relaxed. This is the hypnotic version. Using the 1st Recognition will gently guide you into hypnosis. Repeating it while in the hypnotic state reinforces the suggestion more effectively. I will go through this again in a little more detail.

The second general use of a Recognition is to use it with your eyes open in your normal state of consciousness. Among hypnotists, we call this affirmation. It is merely the practice of repeating a suggestion to yourself in the normal waking state. This tends to reinforce the hypnotic suggestion (but not as powerfully as when repeated in hypnosis). A good time to do this is when you are doing routine tasks that do not require your full attention.

Another good time to use a Recognition as an affirmation is as a thought-stopping mechanism. If you find yourself thinking thoughts that are not in your best interest, you can always stop them by instantly replacing them with any of the Recognitions. Since they are based on simple truths, they are easily acceptable to the deepest parts of you and will tend to have a calming effect. If for some reason you don't agree that a particular Recognition is based in truth, then ask the hypnotist to explain it further. And then if for some reason it does not seem right to you, just skip it for now, and proceed without it until you can talk more about it with your 7th Path Self-Hypnosis® Teacher.

Using the Recognitions in hypnosis

Human beings have a natural tendency to go into and out of hypnosis. It is mainly a state of focused attention that allows for critical factor bypass. And, as I have said before, we have all experienced hypnosis hundreds, if not thousands of times, while driving, watching television, reading a book or just being totally involved in any activity.

While in these naturally induced instances of hypnosis, you may have been hypnotized by your focus on the activity that you were attending to (like driving or watching a movie). If something really important happens you can automatically take your attention away from it and you emerge; this is also true when you do self-hypnosis. If something important comes up while you are doing your 7th Path Self-Hypnosis®, you would simply and easily redirect your attention away from the Recognitions and you would emerge. After this, your attention would go to whatever needed to be done.

It's like the driver who drives the same route every day, she often experiences highway hypnosis. But if someone drifts into her lane, she would instantly respond by stepping on the brake or whatever was appropriate at that time.

This is also true when you do self-hypnosis, whether it is a conventional version, or the 7th Path™ method. It seems that there is always a higher level of awareness functioning. The protective part of you is constantly on the lookout for anything that needs your immediate attention. This does not mean that you should be careless. If you are sitting on your couch at home practicing the 7th Path™ and someone knocks on your front door, you would notice and respond accordingly. You would be more responsive than if you had been napping and had just awakened. Hypnosis is not sleep. Sleep is a state of unconsciousness, while hypnosis is a state of focused consciousness.

Let me talk more about using affirmations. Using affirmations means that you are simply saying positive statements to yourself in the normal state of waking consciousness. For example, when you are doing other things that are routine, you can simply say the Recognitions to yourself. You must have the intent to go into hypnosis for the Recognitions to take you into hypnosis.

As for using the Recognitions in your car in the form of affirmations, I have to say that I do not recommend it for everyone. Someone might get into an accident and then she might say, "Well, I read a book on self-hypnosis and it said that it was safe." I have used affirmations while driving and so have others, but I cannot say that it is perfectly safe for you to do so while driving. Remember that using affirmations does not involve inducing a hypnotic state through any kind of hypnotic induction. Using the Recognitions as affirmations is merely a way of reinforcing the suggestions that you give yourself while in hypnosis, but doing it without the use of hypnosis. Don't do anything that would distract yourself from what you are doing when you are driving or using machinery.

If you have any reservations or concerns at all about using the process of 7th Path™ while your eyes are open then don't do it. You are ultimately responsible for your safety and behavior. But you should be able to repeat the Recognitions in the normal waking state while doing other things, such as your household duties or when you are getting ready for work each day.

Here are some general guidelines for using 7th Path™:

- Commit time, about 5 to 10 minutes (minimum) twice a day for the first week (once in the morning and once in the afternoon or evening).

- After the first week, commit at least 10 minutes twice a day.

- After you have established a routine you can do 20 minutes twice a day, but at least 10 minutes twice a day for about 4 to 6 weeks.

- Find a quiet place where you are unlikely to be interrupted.

- Set a time and use all of the time. If you set 10 minutes aside, use all of the 10 minutes.

- Say the Recognition to yourself. Other thoughts will be generated. This is good.

- Peeking is okay. If you forget the Recognition, it's okay to have them written down.

- Going longer than you intended is okay if you want to.

- Sometimes you will feel very relaxed and sometimes you won't.

- Use the Recognition exactly as given. Don't change the wording at all.

- Decide *when* you are going to do it, and make an appointment with yourself.

- In addition to the morning and afternoon or evening sessions, always do 7th Path Self-Hypnosis® as you go to sleep each night.

Now let me explain each of those guidelines in more depth.
Commit a few minutes three times a day to really making your life better

Let's get this into perspective. Two minutes equals a short commercial break when you are watching TV, ten minutes equals about five commercial breaks. It is not really that long. Twenty-minute sessions are even better. In fact, we have observed that 20 minutes of practice is the optimum period for most people, for their morning and afternoon/evening practice sessions.

Let's look at it this way: you probably want to make some beneficial changes in your life or you would not have read this far and you have probably only had limited success with whatever you tried in the past. Make a deal with yourself. Make a time-limited commitment here to really give this a good chance to work for you. This is what I am talking about: make an agreement with yourself that you will do this process for four to six weeks. Arrange it so that you can do it twice a day and at bedtime. I will tell you more about doing 7th Path™ at bedtime.

Commit 10 to 20 minutes twice a day (a minimum of 5 minutes per practice period the first week when you are using only the 1st Recognition). But make a promise to yourself that if for some reason, something really comes up and you could not do it when you planned to, you will still take this time for yourself. Maybe it will be a little later than you planned to, but you still get your time in. This way you will make the best progress.

I tell my students to consider this: What if it was going to take 200 to 500 minutes of 7th Path Self-Hypnosis® to get rid of the old programs that are getting in the way of your success? How fast do you want to clear away that old programming? Do you want to do get those 200 to 500 minutes done 5, 10, 15 or 20 minutes at a time? Obviously, the more time that you practice the techniques at any given sitting, the faster you will move through baggage and empty your cup. How long it takes to empty your cup is different for each individual.

Chapter 6
The Experience of Doing the Path

What will it feel like? This varies a great deal from session to session and from practitioner to practitioner. The most common experiences are that of a deep state of relaxation and/or emotional release. However, there will also be times when you may feel uncomfortable, physically or emotionally. Both of these results indicate that you are doing the process correctly. The experience of deep relaxation becomes more common after you have emptied the cup somewhat.

Look forward to the extremely relaxing sessions, as they will be very nice and have a tendency to revitalize or re-energize you. But the uncomfortable experiences are just as important, and for some people, they are even more important. When you are feeling uncomfortable (i.e., antsy or fidgety) or even experiencing strong emotions (i.e., sadness, anger or fearfulness) you are clearing out those old feelings that have gotten in the way. You are experiencing the emptying of the cup. *Often practitioners who are in this phase do not feel hypnotized.* If this happens to you, do not worry about it. Just keep on with the process. Hypnosis is not relaxation.

If, for some reason, you experience ongoing strong emotional reactions, I recommend that you meet with a qualified hypnotherapist or other mental health professional (trained in this process) for some individual work. Working with the hypnotherapist will greatly increase the speed at which you get through the process and get on to the more positive programming that comes along with the 5th Recognition.

If at any time you decide that you want to work with a hypnotherapist and accelerate your progress, there is a process that we call 5-PATH®, a type of hypnotherapy, which influenced the early development of 7th Path Self-Hypnosis®. If you choose to do the two simultaneously, you will move through the process of "emptying the cup" more quickly. As I mentioned before, you can visit our web sites or call our office to find out if a 7th Path Self-Hypnosis® Teacher or 5-PATH® Hypnotherapist is in your area.

Also, if you find that you are having trouble maintaining the daily discipline of doing 7th Path Self-Hypnosis® on your own, then you may find it useful to work directly with a 5-PATH® Certified Hypnotherapist who is also a 7th Path Self-Hypnosis® Teacher. She can help you to stay focused on what you are doing while supporting your efforts to maintain a good daily routine of doing 7th Path Self-Hypnosis®.

Back to what practicing 7th Path Self-Hypnosis® can feel like. If you are tired and you do this process you may fall asleep. This is because the practice tends to be relaxing and interrupts the kinds of thoughts that would tend to keep you awake. Doing the 7th Path™, at night when you are in bed usually puts an end to almost any kind of sleep difficulties.

How will I know if I am doing it right?

This is an incredibly simple process. Here it is in a nutshell: say the Recognition to yourself and then wait for the Echo to come. We use the term "Echo," to refer to any experience that you have after you have said a Recognition to yourself when doing 7th Path Self-Hypnosis®. These experiences include thoughts, feelings, sensations, memories and mental pictures which come from inside of you. As soon as you are aware that you are experiencing such an Echo, go back to saying the Recognition to yourself. *If you are doing that, you are doing everything correctly, and anything that occurs during the practice session is perfect.*

While you are doing that, you will probably go into hypnosis in a minute or two. You may also feel very relaxed as this occurs. This is nice. But relaxation in and of itself does not mean that you are in hypnosis. It does not mean that you are doing the process either right or wrong. *Relaxation is simply something that tends to happen while you do the practice of the 7th Path. The only criteria for determining whether or not you are doing things correctly, is whether or not you are doing the two steps: say the Recognition to yourself and then wait for the Echo. Do not try to determine if you are in hypnosis or how deep you are.*

Some people report seeing colors, or feeling light, or heavy, or tingling, etc. These experiences are common, but not required. Often people will feel a sudden jerk in one of their limbs. This is common and I take it as a good sign. Your body is probably just letting go of stress, and that is a very nice thing.

How do I emerge?

The most important point regarding the emerging process is that you can emerge from this process any time you want to. You will automatically emerge if there is anything that needs your attention. Your protective function is always working. When you want to emerge from hypnosis just stop what you are doing and open your eyes.

After you have been practicing the techniques for the time you have set aside, simply and slowly prepare to open your eyes. You can simply do this by consciously opening your eyes. Some practitioners like to do a little count up from one to three or one to five before they open their eyes. Any of the above will do fine. Just do it with respect for the state you are in. If you are feeling extremely relaxed then give yourself a few moments to fully emerge so that it is comfortable for you. Don't just open your eyes and jump out of your chair. Treat the emerging process in the same way you approach awakening; like you have just had a little catnap. Make it a comfortable thing.

What if I'm interrupted?

Interruptions are unavoidable, it seems. Someone might come to the door, or there might be a noise in the other room that you want to check out. When and if this happens, gently open your eyes and take care of the interruption and then go back to doing the process.

Since you are not asleep, you will be aware of what is going on around you. Your "protective part" will be listening to hear if it is anything important. If it is something important, just take care of it; if it is not important, then just keep on with the process.

How to use the Recognitions when you are going to sleep

Use the process when you go to sleep at night. Nighttime is one of the three times a day that you do this (two times during the day and when you go to sleep at night). This is the easiest time to use the process. If you are one of those individuals who has trouble getting to sleep, you will probably love this part of your daily practice because regular use of the Recognitions tends to cause you to go to sleep more quickly. This process is both relaxing and tends to interrupt the thought-following (mind chatter) that has kept you awake in the past.

One note of advice: If you find that doing the process at night keeps you awake, then you can stop doing it for awhile, perhaps for a week or so. Continue doing 7th Path™ during the day. You are probably just going through a phase of emotional clearing. When the daytime sessions become relaxing, return to using the techniques at night. If you don't want to stop doing 7th Path™ at bedtime, continue doing the bedtime session, but only use the 1st Recognition (unless it also keeps you awake, but this is usually not the case). This approach often works well because the 1st Recognition seems to be the one that brings the most comfort to people.

Longer periods are okay as well

Many practitioners have reported that doing the techniques for more than 20 minutes at a time can be a very useful experience. I totally agree. Sometimes on a Sunday afternoon when I have some time, I enjoy luxuriously setting aside up to an hour and a half for doing the 7th Path™ Recognitions. It can be really wonderful. You can achieve levels of relaxation that go far beyond what you may have experienced in your 10 to 20 minute sessions.

Also, if you are going through a period of emotional clearing, doing a longer period of 7th Path™ can be very beneficial. You can really let emotions go during one of these longer sessions. Just go to bed and let it all go.

If you fall asleep during an extended daytime session, that is all right. During a longer period of practice, I have napped off and on, always going back to the Recognitions when I awake.

I have also found that using a very simple tapping technique can be very useful in moving practitioners through an emotional period more quickly. The process is called *7th Path Tapping™*. If you feel that an emotional or physical discomfort gets "stuck" in your body and is not moving after persisting for a couple of days of practice of 7th Path Self-Hypnosis, you can tap directly on that location *as you say* the Recognition that provoked the discomfort to that point in your body (the Sending Point). For specific instructions on how to do this, talk to your hypnotherapist or 7th Path™ Teacher about using this technique. Note, this is not EFT. In this technique there is only one tapping point.

Use the Recognition exactly as given - Do not change the wording at all

Each Recognition is worded in a very specific way; each word has a purpose. If you don't feel comfortable with a word, speak with your hypnotherapist about it. He or she may know of an alternative word that can be used instead. However, in most cases, the discomfort that you have with the way the Recognition is written is part of the process. The Recognition is likely to be resonating with something in your past, which means it is working and you are doing it right. When a Recognition results in an uncomfortable feeling, it is called dissonance. When you can go through all of the Recognitions on a regular basis without experiencing any dissonance, you have accomplished a great deal. You have cleaned out a great deal of negativity and stress. At this point you should seek to learn the Full Forms if you do not already have them. Once you have learned the Full Forms, you are encouraged to continue the journey by also learning and using the Ultimate Recognitions.

Do not change wording to make it more comfortable. Some clients think that they are "saying" the same thing, but doing it in "their own words." They report that it is more comfortable for them to do the process with different wording. Do not paraphrase the Recognitions or change the wording in any way. If you do, then you are changing the meaning. When you reword the Recognitions you are changing the vibrational quality of the Recognitions and changing its affect. Poorly written hypnotic suggestions can be completely ineffective or have the opposite affect from what is intended!

What kind of results should I expect? How long will it take?

The experience of doing 7th Path Self-Hypnosis® varies a great deal from one person to the next, and so does how fast an individual experiences results. Most people will notice a difference in how they are feeling after a few days or a week or so (more calm, patient, less stressed, etc.), and some will find that it takes longer. Regular use of the first four Recognitions should begin to make you feel more peaceful and relaxed. On the other hand, some individuals who have a great deal of emotional "baggage" to process may find that it takes longer. Nevertheless, they too report feeling more in control and more patient with others.

Most of us who learn to use this system will have to go through an emotional period. After things have calmed down emotionally, and you have used the first four Recognitions for a about a month, it is time to move on to the 5th Recognition. On average the emotional clearing takes from two to four weeks, depending on your dedication to the process and your own personal history. As you do this, focus on the idea of how much better you will feel once you have emptied that cup of old emotions.

Generally speaking, you should practice the 1st Recognition for about one week. Then you should add the 2nd Recognition to your practice periods. This will cause you to go from the minimum practice of 5 minutes per practice session (when only doing the First Recognition) to then doing a minimum of 10 minutes per session (once you have added the Second Recognition).

When you are at the level of having both Recognitions to practice, your intent should be to spend an equal amount of time on each one. You do the 1st Recognition for 5 minutes, or so, and then continue by doing the next Recognition for the remaining 5 minutes. There is no break in the process, just start doing the 2nd Recognition after completing the first 5 minutes of doing the 1st Recognition.

Once you get the 3rd Recognition, this will add another 5 minutes to your minimum practice time, making your total minimum practice time 15 minutes. When you add the 4th Recognition, you add another 5 minutes to your practice time. Keeping in mind that 20 minutes is the optimum practice time, it works out nicely that you have four Recognitions and you are spending 5 minutes on each one.

However, when you have just one Recognition, 5 minutes is your minimum practice time, but 20 minutes is still the optimum. 10 minutes is your minimum amount of time when you have two Recognitions, spending 5 minutes on each one. In any case, 20 minutes is optimum, no matter how many Recognitions you may have.

If you want to get the most out of doing 7th Path Self-Hypnosis® you would take the 20 minute optimum time and divide that by the number or Recognitions that you have and spend that amount of time on each one.

In other words, if you have 1, 2, 3, 4, 5, 6, 7, 8, or 9 Recognitions you divide the 20 minutes by that number and spend that much time on each Recognition during your practice period. (Yes, this is a bit repetitive here, but we get so many questions about this that I am repeating it again to help everyone understand this.)

Here is a table that will also serve to make this minimum vs. optimum time investment concept more clear:

Number of Recognitions	Minimum Time	Optimum Time
1	5 Minutes	20 Minutes
2	10 Minutes	20 Minutes
3	15 Minutes	20 Minutes
4	20 Minutes	20 Minutes
5	20 Minutes	20 Minutes
6	20 Minutes	20 Minutes
7	20 Minutes	20 Minutes
8	20 Minutes	20 Minutes
9	20 Minutes	20 Minutes

The optimum time of 20 minutes is not absolute. It is only a recommendation. If you find that you like to do 20 to 30 minutes, that is wonderful, too. I also like to recommend the use of this kind of progressive working-up-to-it approach shown in the table for beginners. This way you can start with only 5 minutes in each practice period and gradually build up to the longer 20 minute periods as you learn more Recognitions.

Chapter 7
Reprogramming Yourself for Success

After you have done the work of the first four Recognitions, it is time to receive the 5th Recognition. It is the use of the 5th Recognition where we begin to send hypnotic suggestions into the subconscious mind and fill your cup with all the wonderful suggestions that you want. This is where *specific* results would most commonly be measured for any change that has not already spontaneously occurred. (This tends to produce an onset of healthier behaviors, or at least the desire to begin to do these healthy behaviors, including eating right, exercising regularly, giving up poisons in the form of tobacco and unnecessary or recreational drugs, etc.)

This book only contains wording of the 1st Recognition

All of the Recognitions are given for the first time while in hypnosis with the exception of the first. As I mentioned before, the wording of the 1st Recognition is learned in the regular waking state (not in hypnosis) because it is helpful in explaining the process and how to use the techniques. Disclosing the 1st Recognition in the "waking" state also helps to build trust as it reveals what the rest of the Recognitions would be like.

Much can be accomplished with the 1st Recognition. If the 1st Recognition was all that you ever learned and practiced (for the time recommended, in the way that you are instructed), you would probably benefit a great deal. However, it is recommended that you receive and use at least the first five Recognitions to begin with. You start off by doing them in the Short Forms, and then progress to use them in the Full Forms. They were designed to work together as a set. These first five are called the Basic Recognitions. The next four are the Advanced Recognitions.

There are more Recognitions if you want them (9 total); having them will speed up your progress and help you to achieve even more. The additional Recognitions, beyond the Basic Recognitions, are for ongoing development, which is intended to help you to continue to reduce stress, gain a more positive outlook, and ultimately develop your human potential. They are also very useful for those who want to develop in a spiritual manner. These Advanced Recognitions help you to see life and its purpose from a higher perspective. If you are not sure if the Advanced Recognitions are for you, I suggest that you go ahead and get the 6th Recognition and try it out for a few days. If it does not suit your current needs, you can always discontinue its use. I find, however, that most people who chose to start using the 6th Recognition decide that they want to get more, at least up to the 9th Recognition. If you are one of those practioners who is not interested in that sort of thing—that is perfectly okay; enjoy the Basic Recognitions. You will accomplish a great deal by using only them. They are yours to use for as long as you care to. I will discuss each of the Recognitions later in the book so you have more information on each one.

There are two forms of each of the Recognitions, a Short Form and the Full Form. Each Recognition is first given in the Short Form because the short forms are the easiest and simplest to learn and use. After you have received the first five Recognitions in the Short Forms, you may receive the full versions if you like, as their use will *speed things along*.

The Full Form of the 4th Recognition is a perfect example of how the extended version of the Recognition takes the message deeper into you and gives it a much broader meaning. This is why the Full Form of the 4th Recognition is usually given before any of the other Full Forms.

The Full Form of the 1st through the 3rd Recognitions, while not required, tend to speed up the process and cause the Recognitions to benefit you more fully when you are ready for them. (They will certainly make the process more interesting for most of you!) Also, the complete versions tend to improve your ability to utilize the Recognitions throughout your life.

Without the Full Forms, some practitioners may apply the benefits of the Recognitions only to the area or issues in their life that brought them in to do the work. The Full Forms of the Recognitions truly make the process more holistic in their effect. Once you have received a Full Form, this will be much more evident to you.

Once you have received the Full Forms of the first five Recognitions, you can learn and begin using the Advance Recognitions, again first in the Short Forms, then in the Full Forms. When you have learned and used all of the Full Recognitions, and have done so for a minimum of two weeks, you may learn the Ultimate Recognitions.

How do I get more Recognitions?

As explained above, this book only contains the 1st Recognition. Where do you get the others? In most cases, you can get them from the same source as this book. If you are working with a 7th Path™ Teacher or 5-PATH® Hypnotherapist, she can give you more Recognitions. All 7th Path™ Recognitions are received in hypnosis. This is why you will need to get with a qualified 7th Path™ Teacher or hypnotherapist (live or through a recording of a class). She will guide you back into hypnosis and give you the next recognition in the short form or Full Version. Receiving of the Recognitions requires special hypnotic processes or techniques. Think of it as software for the mind that needs to be "installed" so that your mind can use it properly. The Recognitions need to be initiated or started in a specific way to receive the maximum benefit from them.

Because the Recognitions are taught while the recipient is in hypnosis it is necessary that only a properly trained and certified 7th Path Self-Hypnosis® Teacher teach this process. That is why it is important that you do not share these Recognitions with anyone. If you simply told a friend to start saying the Recognitions to herself, you would be doing her and the techniques a disservice.

If you were to tell someone what the Recognition was, and she just started repeating it to herself like a meditation technique, it probably would not work the same way. There may be some benefit, but it would be a poor evaluation of the procedure, and not doing it properly would diminish it. So once again, please do not share the Recognitions with anyone unless you become trained to teach the 7th Path Self-Hypnosis® system. Contact our offices or visit our web site and learn how you can become a 7th Path™ Teacher or 5-PATH® Hypnotist (a college degree is not required).

You can work with any 7th Path™ Teacher or hypnotist you choose to work with. Each one can give you your Recognitions, in short or full form. You do not need to stay with the same person. Also, techniques may be received either in an individual session or in a group environment. Both situations have benefits. Generally, one is not recommended over the other.

The first five Recognitions can be learned through the use of an audio program. It can be purchased by visiting the website, *www.7thPathSelfHypnosis.com* or by calling our office at (469) 969-2176 or toll free at (800) 965-3390.

Chapter 8
More Information about the Recognitions and How to Use Them

I learned my Recognitions a little differently from my friend, who also learned the 7th Path™ Recognitions. Who is right?

The 7th Path Self-Hypnosis® system was not discovered written in an ancient scroll somewhere. It was not written in stone either. It is a result of experience from conducting thousands of 5-PATH® hypnosis sessions, and a good dose of inspiration.

The 7th Path Self-Hypnosis® system is not a result of scientists working in a laboratory or university – although, I would love to have the opportunity to take a more scientific approach in studying the results which have been reported by those using the 7th Path Self-Hypnosis® system. Unfortunately, true science and empiricism is slow and laborious. I could not wait for the opportunity to do that kind of methodical examination of the process before offering it to those interested; this process has proved itself time and again in individual hypnotherapeutic situations as well as in classrooms around the world.

There are older versions out there. They are good and have worked for others. We constantly strive to improve the system which has caused a change in wording here and there since the earliest days in the development of the system (though no changes in wording have occurred in almost 10 years). If your friend received her Recognitions way back then and they are different from the ones you are receiving, she can update her Recognitions at any time.

On the other hand, it is more likely that something else has occurred. Some people have either accidentally or purposefully changed the wording of the Recognitions over time. Ask your friend if she wrote the Recognitions down when they were first given. If you ask a 7th Path™ Instructor if the version that is different from yours is correct, she may not be able to validate an older version of the Recognitions. We do not teach our 7th Path™ Teachers the old versions, only the new ones. Therefore, if the Recognitions have changed, the 7th Path™ Teacher or hypnotherapist will have the newest versions. There is no charge for validating or updating a Recognition.

Basically, using the old versions is fine, but changing the wording by accident or on purpose is not. Of course, we cannot control what everyone is doing with our Recognitions. We can only say that if you change the wording of any Recognition, or use them differently than we teach you, then you are not doing the 7th Path Self-Hypnosis®.

How to use the Recognitions with the Delta (Δ) word

Now I am going to go into a bit more detail about how to actually do 7th Path Self-Hypnosis®. In review, let me remind you that each Recognition has two parts, the *Delta Part* and the *Suggestion Part.*

First, let me discuss the Delta word which makes up the Delta Part. The symbol "Δ" or the word "Delta", is sometimes used in math and science to represent change, such as in a variable in a formula or algebraic expression of some kind, or even in Calculus! We have adopted the "Δ" symbol to represent your highest source of positive change in your life. The Delta word is just exactly the same as a blank space in a fill-in-the-blank sentence or question. For instance, we have all taken exams where you are asked to fill in the blank. Here is a very simple example: "One plus one equals _____." Here you would fill in the blank with the answer.

The use of the Delta word is a very important part of the 7th Path Self-Hypnosis® system. The Delta word (or concept) represents your highest concept related to your power to change--or, your Higher Power, etc. Since this is so important to what we are doing, it is out of respect for your highest ideals and concepts that we use a replaceable symbol, in this case, "Delta". Simply using a "_____" or blank is not quite as respectful. You should not actually say the word "Delta" when doing the Recognitions; it should always be replaced by something more powerful.

Here are some further examples of how it could be used. (*These are not Recognitions.*)

> I call my Higher Power _____(Delta).
> I call my Higher Power Nature.
> I call my Higher Power God.
> I call my Higher Power The Goddess.
> I call my Higher Power The Tao.
> I call my Higher Power The Force.
> I call my Higher Power Family.
> I call my Higher Power Love.
> I call my Higher Power Christ.
> I call my Higher Power Buddha.
> I call my Higher Power Allah.
> I call my Higher Power The Infinite.
> I call my Higher Power The Universe and All That Is!.

As you can see by the above examples, the Delta word (or concept) can be replaced by any idea, philosophy, or principle that you believe will be helpful in your goal to make good, positive improvements in your life.

By far the most common Delta word used among our clients is "God." But it is always up to you, and if you wish, you can keep your Delta word private. You don't have to tell anyone what it is, and you can change it at any time. You can also use a different Delta word for each Recognition if you so choose. The 7th Path Self-Hypnosis® system is very flexible and forgiving. From time to time, your teacher may ask you to tell her what your Delta word is. We recommend that you do so as she is just checking to make sure you understand the process.

As you already know, the 1st Recognition is given to you in the normal waking consciousness state of mind so that it can be used to explain the process. Then, after you go into hypnosis, the Recognition is given to you again with instructions on how to use it to re-enter hypnosis.

The simple process of doing 7th Path Self-Hypnosis®

Basically, this is how the process works: you will set aside some time to do the 7th Path; get yourself in a comfortable position (any position will do as long as it is comfortable for you); and do whatever you need to do to reduce the chances of being interrupted (turn off the telephone, put your dog or cat in another room, etc.).

Then simply close your eyes and begin to use the Recognition in this way:

1. Say the Recognition silently to yourself. Don't say it out loud.
2. Wait until you experience the Echo. Any thought, feeling, sensation, memory or picture.
3. Go back to step 1.

That is all there is to it. It is very simple.

Whenever you use the 1st Recognition with the intent of going into hypnosis, you will go back into hypnosis. The subconscious mind will then receive the Recognition as a hypnotic suggestion. It will be reinforced over and over again during the time that you do the practice.

Sometimes, you will be in hypnosis and not think you are. This is a very common experience. Don't worry whether or not you are in hypnosis, or how deeply you have gone into the hypnotic state. Just accept that you are or that you soon will be.

What if you don't go into hypnosis some times? The worst thing that can happen is that you could spend the time and not be in hypnosis. In that case, you will be doing affirmations (which are about as close to hypnosis as you can get, and some professionals even categorize the use of affirmations as a form of hypnosis).

Worrying is not part of the process! So don't worry about whether or not you are in hypnosis, or how deep you are in hypnosis. Worrying can only add stress and slow down the process. Believe me; if you do as instructed, the chances are very, very good that you will achieve the effects that you desire. I have never received a report of anyone doing this process correctly and not experiencing positive results.

Let me talk a little more about the other Echoes that will come up. After you say the Recognition to yourself, wait, and it will resonate through you and produce the Echo, usually in the form of thoughts, feelings, sensations, memories or pictures. Do not follow the stream of thoughts. Just be aware that you have experienced the Echo (i.e., thought about something) and go back to the Recognition. You do not need to do anything with the Echo. Don't analyze it. Don't think any more of it. Just go back to the Recognition.

Let me tell you what I mean by "don't follow the thoughts (or other Echoes)". After you say the Recognition silently to yourself, wait, and something will happen. We call that the Echo: the thought, feeling, sensation, memory or picture, which comes into your awareness after you say the Recognition to yourself. Usually it only takes a second or so. Sometimes it takes longer. If it takes more than a couple of seconds, just enjoy the moment of peace while you're waiting, and the Echo will come. When the Echo comes, just return to the Recognition (repeat the Recognition to yourself again). Do not say the Recognition again until you have experienced the Echo.

If you allow yourself to follow the Echo, you are not doing the process as well as if you were to immediately return to the Recognition (by saying it again to yourself). For example, if while you were doing 7th Path Self-Hypnosis® and you thought, "I wonder if I should go to the store today," that would be a thought which is an Echo. Right after that thought (Echo), you just go back to the Recognition by saying the Recognition to yourself again, and so on.

However, if you were to start thinking about the advantages or disadvantages of going to the store, then that is what we call "thought following". You are just generating your same old stream of consciousness, and you are not doing 7th Path Self-Hypnosis® any longer, just sitting there thinking like you always do. If you catch yourself doing this, welcome to the "club;" we have all done that. It is not a major error. Just take your attention back to the Recognition. With practice, you will do less and less "thought following".

The Echoes that you have will fall into three general categories: positive, neutral and negative. Let me start off by discussing the nature of Neutral Echoes. Neutral Echoes are just busy thoughts that we all have every day which are neither positive nor negative in nature. It seems that to some extent that the mind works by association. If I ask you to respond with the first word that comes to your mind; when I say "salt," you might say "pepper." The two things are just strongly associated in our minds.

Here are some other common associations:

1. Night and day.
2. Dogs and cats.
3. Up and down.
4. In and out.

These associations are neither positive nor negative in value; they are just neutral associations we have stored in our subconscious minds. On the other hand, if your mind is concerned with something else, other thoughts might come up; thoughts that are associated with what is on your mind.

For example, if you were really hungry now, our association experiment might go something like this:

1. <u>Night</u> and dinner.
2. <u>Dogs</u> and wieners.
3. <u>Up</u> and go eat.
4. <u>In</u> and take out.

Other neutral thoughts are busy thoughts which happen to cross your mind. They have to do with what is going on in your life right now or are expected in your immediate future. Some of the thoughts that you have when you do this process can be very mundane for a while. These non-emotional, mundane thoughts are also part of the process.

There are two other categories that are more important in the process because the Recognitions will use them and resonate with them. Those are "negative" and "positive" Echoes. The 7th Path™ Recognition is, in itself, a positive thought. So, because of the way the mind works (by association), the Recognition may generate positive Echoes in the form of thoughts, feelings, sensations, memories or pictures. "One good thing can lead to another," as they say.

Our minds also associate by contrast. For example if I say "hot," you might say "cold" or I might say "good," and you would say "bad." Negative associations can be generated from a positive statement. I could say "innocent" and you might say "guilty." This is what happens when you experience negative Echoes.

One last example, I might say, "heaven" and you might say "hell," and so it goes with the human mind. Whether your Echoes are neutral, positive or negative, exciting or dull, they are all a useful part of the process. Just become an objective observer of each Echo. It will be a very interesting process for most of you.

Chapter 9
The Basic Recognitions

In this chapter I will discuss each of the Basic Recognitions individually. I'll give you any special instructions or insights that you need right now.

The 1st Recognition

I am now going to discuss the 1st Recognition. This is the only Recognition that will be discussed in this much detail before you receive it in hypnosis. This is the Short Form. As you know by now, there is also a Full Form, but that is not given until you have worked with the short form for awhile, usually at least a week.

"Delta renews my life."

This is a positive suggestion or thought because it suggests change in a most positive way. It suggests renewal at the highest and healthiest level. If Delta had anything to do with it, any changes would be healthy and positive. Choose your Delta word wisely. It should contain the highest vibration that you can think of and hold in your mind for that Recognition.

This suggestion may generate other positive Echoes in the form of thoughts of renewal. Such positive thoughts might include thinking about how you would like your life to change, or how that change might make you feel. It might be a thought that is hopeful, etc. These are all positive thoughts. You can immediately see that using the Recognition can increase the number of positive thoughts you experience in a day. This can also positively affect your mood and optimism.

Also, the Recognition may generate negative thoughts. Negative thoughts are the kinds of thoughts that make you feel uncomfortable and cause your mood to fall. Negative thoughts tend to be limiting and self-defeating. It is for the most part, the negative thoughts that have been holding you back from making real headway in your life, or in the particular area that you want to improve (i.e., changing unhealthy habits and behaviors).

When you do the 7th Path™ practice, you are constantly introducing the Recognitions which are positive thoughts. When the positive thoughts "bump" into the negative beliefs and concepts, they can generate an uncomfortable feeling. This is because of the dissonance between the positive meaning of the Recognition and the negative programming in your nervous system. Through the repetition of the Recognitions, the negative thoughts are first weakened, then neutralized, and finally replaced by a positive thought, belief or concept.

Sometimes you may have the experience of feeling the negative energy or emotion "move" through you and be released. This can be uncomfortable. Some will cry or feel antsy, or even get angry. In this case you are experiencing the old programming being removed. You are literally letting go of the past.

You are not encouraged to try to understand why that old situation happened; just return to the Recognition. The feelings associated with those memories were based in error and now you are fixing those misperceptions.

It seems that somehow, at a subconscious level, the negativity is rejected as it is reevaluated in the light of the Recognition, and seen as false. This seems to be similar to the operation of the critical factor (the comparing function) of the mind, but working in reverse. (See the previous discussion regarding what hypnosis is, i.e., bypass of the critical factor of the conscious mind.)

In normal waking consciousness, the critical factor compares new incoming information with existing information in the subconscious mind (where your beliefs are stored). If the new information does not match the beliefs, then the new information is not considered to be valid information. Your mind may place that kind of information in a holding place, what I call an "anomaly file," which is part of the subconscious mind that holds all data (whether it fits into your beliefs or not). It still knows about that information, it just doesn't believe it.

Remember that using 7th Path™ is a system of self-hypnosis; we turn the tables on the critical factor. Since the 7th Path™ system is uniquely hypnotic and suggestive in nature, this causes the negative thoughts to be weakened and eventually neutralized or totally rejected.

This is like the critical factor working in reverse. Because of the hypnotic nature of the practice, the critical factor is bypassed; the suggestions find the negative thoughts and go to work on them. Two interesting things seem to happen. One is that the negative thought is activated by the Recognition (through association, also called resonance) which brings it into subconscious or even conscious awareness (such as when old memories associated with the feeling come to mind).

The erroneous belief may be subconsciously or consciously evaluated in the light of the new suggestion and adult awareness, then the negative thought is rejected if it cannot hold up to the current information. This subconscious process is sometimes observed in dreams. Often, 7th Path Self-Hypnosis® Practitioners report that their dreams become more vivid and that they tend to be more likely to remember them.

Remember that much of this negative programming may have occurred while you were just a child. These negative thoughts or beliefs about yourself or the world have not been critically examined since then. (Often the situation in which the programming occurred has been long since forgotten, meaning not retrievable through conscious effort, but can be retrieved through hypnosis.)

Once the negative thought is activated by the Recognition, it becomes subject to newer (adult) perceptions, analysis, or suggestions that are being given at the time (which are positive in nature). This process causes a collapse of the old, limiting thoughts and associated feelings.

The Recognitions are like antacids: they work on contact. No conscious work needs to be done. Just say the Recognition and wait for the Echo.

As a result of removing the old programming (which caused the unconscious mind to produce feelings of anxiety and stress), there tends to be a constant shift toward calm, confidence, and optimism for the 7th Path™ Practitioner.

Let me show you how this works. In the illustration which follows, I show the 1st Recognition, which is a positive thought. It generates all three kinds of thoughts: positive, negative, or neutral. These Echoes are then combined with the Recognition through association (by simply being thought of at approximately the same time).

Here is a diagram of how the process works.

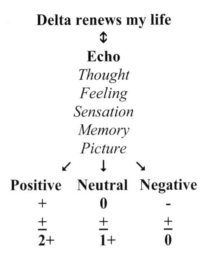

To explain this further, the Recognition is a positive suggestion and thought. When the Recognition generates a positive thought, they add together to equal two positive thoughts (a positive and a positive = two positive thoughts, or 2+).

When the use of a Recognition generates a neutral thought, the two combine and add together to equal one positive thought (a zero and a positive = one positive thought or 1+).

In the third case, the use of the Recognition may generate a negative thought (dissonance). The Recognitions, which are positive thoughts, combine with the negative thought and tends to neutralize them (a positive and a negative = 0).

The net result is a move or shift toward more positive thinking which can lead to feeling more positive mentally, physically and emotionally.

What happens here is the reinforcement of positive thinking and feeling, which is, of course, a good thing. Note how this is different from just listening to some tape of a motivational speaker.

When the motivational speaker talks to you, you only feel better for a short period of time. In the long run, most of what is being said will be rejected by the critical factor and what was said does not become a belief. His speech never really makes a dent in the subconscious mind. But this process is working at the subconscious level of the mind, removing the old beliefs. With that done, now you can listen to the motivational speaker, and because the information in the subconscious mind is not in opposition to what is being heard (i.e., how capable you are and how if you apply yourself you can do it, etc.), you can take the information and use it. It doesn't get rejected. So after you have used the 7th Path Self-Hypnosis® system to remove the old programming, any other self-improvement program that you choose to involve yourself in will work a whole lot better than it did before. All of that positive information will just become more believable, and therefore, more doable and sustainable!

Remember, there is also something going on that may be unique to this system of self-hypnosis. The Recognitions serve to ferret out old negative thoughts and feelings. Over time, these feelings are activated by the Recognition and neutralized. This leaves the subconscious free of the old limiting thoughts, beliefs and feelings associated with them. The subconscious mind is turned into fertile ground for the planting and acceptance of new suggestions, which you will be able to give to yourself when the 5th Recognition is used in the Full Form.

More about the 1st Recognition

Each of the first five Recognitions are closely related to the 5-PATH® system of hypnotherapy. The first phase of 5-PATH® is directed at getting the client started. We want the client to have a positive experience with hypnosis, and to have a hopeful experience overall. The theme of the 1st Recognition is that of hope and starting anew.

When you receive the 1st Recognition, write it here for reference in both the Short Form and the Full Form as you get each version.

_____

_____

_____

_____

This Recognition is designed to connect you with your Delta. It is our experience that long-lasting change occurs most often if the process used to make the change has a spiritual component. In addition to the 1st Recognition being a hypnotic induction, deepening and suggestion procedure, it is also both an invocation for—and an invitation to—your Higher Power to be part of this healing process.

All of the Recognitions given in this book are in their Short Form. There are complete forms of the Recognitions as I explained above. Teachers only give the short forms because they are easier to use and require less of an adjustment at subconscious levels. For many people, the Full Form of the Recognitions would simply be too large a step to take.

Your therapist or 7th Path™ Teacher will probably speak with you about the Full Forms. Getting and using the Full Forms are recommended to move more quickly toward your goals. They also deepen, quicken or broaden the process, which of course are all good things to do.

As always, please feel free to ask your therapist or 7th Path™ Teacher any questions that come to mind. Also, remember that if you are not comfortable with spirituality you can use terms like "love," "family," etc. for your Delta word.

All in all, we get a great deal from just four little words: "Delta renews my life." They work together in this process to be seven things:

1. A *hypnotic induction*, because they take you back into hypnosis.

2. A *hypnotic deepening technique*, because repeating them takes you deeper into hypnosis.

3. A *hypnotic suggestion*, because used in hypnosis they suggest a positive change.

4. An *invitation* for your highest beliefs or Higher Power to be a part of this process.

5. An *invocation* of that power because that which we focus on tends to be increased in our lives.

6. An *affirmation*, because you can use it when you are not in hypnosis.

7. And if you wish, you could even call it a *Meditation* or a *Prayer*.

This list of *seven* is one of the reasons that this process is called 7th Path™. This system of self-hypnosis was not named 7th Path Self-Hypnosis® because of the number of Recognitions; there are nine Recognitions.

The 2nd Recognition

In the 5-PATH® system of hypnotherapy, our clients are helped to experience a connection with who they are. This is the real you. Imagine becoming who you really are as if you grew without all of that negative programming.

When you receive the 2nd Recognition, write it here for reference in both the Short Form and the Full Form as you get each version.

_____

_____

_____

_____

So it is with the 2nd Recognition; it is designed to remove all barriers to knowing how really loveable you are despite what others may have thought, said, or done to you in your life. It is this false programming that leads the child that you once were into a state of fear, shyness, or insecurity about herself. It does not matter where it came from; it only needs to be eliminated so that new, more positive thoughts, beliefs, and feelings can be accepted.

This change affects so much in your life. How you experience your present state of affairs or how you expect your future to turn out is a direct reflection of your experiences in the past. It is your past experiences that have shaped who you are in this moment. Unfortunately, your first beliefs came from the experiences of a child that you once were and, as a child, you did not have the kind of maturity and understanding of the world that you have now. Those initial pieces of programming are based on the perceptions of a child! Boy, if we only knew then what we know now! Imagine how that would have or could have changed our earliest perceptions that have led to our beliefs about ourselves and the world.

As erroneous programming is rejected and new, more realistic and positive thoughts and beliefs are instilled, you begin to experience your present in a more realistic way, and your expectations regarding the future become more positive. Furthermore, your expectations, whether positive or negative, have an impact on what you experience now and eventually experience in the future.

A person with a significant level of negative expectations in mind regarding any particular area of her life tends to have just those kinds of experiences! Conversely, people who have positive and optimistic expectations tend to realize those experiences in life and are generally more successful at whatever they set out to do. Furthermore, like attracts like, and as they say, "birds of a feather flock together," and so on. When you hold negative thoughts and feelings inside, you will tend to attract more people, situations and events that hold that kind of vibration, or at least reinforce that kind of thinking and feeling. This 2nd Recognition will work to set you free from those negative attraction energies.

The 3rd Recognition

The 3rd Recognition is an important extension of the 2nd Recognition; it is designed to powerfully move you forward in self-acceptance and self-esteem.

When you receive the 3rd Recognition, write it here for reference in both the Short Form and the Full Form as you get each version.

_____

_____

_____

_____

This is a Recognition that provides a more thorough removal of erroneous programming from your past. This is programming concerning conscious or subconscious beliefs that have led to feelings of inadequacy in any area of your life. Once this Recognition has been fully absorbed, you will feel confident, worthy, and secure in your everyday life. There is a tendency for your concentration, memory, and outlook to improve tremendously.

So many "self-improvement" programs try to "pump you up" with suggestions of self-confidence, but the effects quickly wear off because those procedures never really address the cause of your lack of self-confidence or esteem: the old programming. These programs simply tell you how great you are. However, as soon as they tell you how much potential you have for success, the critical factor starts working and rejects everything before it can be accepted by the subconscious mind where that information could do you any good. This is what sabotages your ability to make long-term change; those early adopted negative beliefs are protected by your critical factor. This is why this program is so important: this Recognition will find those limiting beliefs and through the use of hypnosis work to neutralize them (hypnosis causes a bypass of the critical factor).

Said in a different way, without the use of hypnosis, the critical factor compares the new information coming in with *all of your past experiences* and says, "Who are you kidding? You're not that good, and if you pretend you are, you will just wind up getting hurt!" So, believing that it is in your best interest, the critical factor goes to work, and sooner or later the good positive suggestions are rejected.

The 3rd Recognition removes the old programming which has prevented you from doing what you needed or wanted to do. The mind becomes fertile ground for these new suggestions to be planted where they can grow rather than be rejected. You can then develop a true sense of self-confidence and self-esteem that will help you to be much more successful at the really important things in your life.

The 4th Recognition

Here, we focus on becoming truly free from the past! Free from anger. Free from guilt. Free from being manipulated by others from our past. Free from old regrets. That is what the 4th Recognition does. What if you were just more patient with others and slower to feel guilty or angry? What if others just couldn't "push your buttons" like they do? Would that change your life? You bet it would!

When you receive the 4th Recognition, write it here for reference in both the Short Form and the Full Form as you get each version.

_____

_____

_____

_____

Imagine how good you could feel if you could completely free yourself from all those old tired feelings of anger and guilt that you have been carrying around inside of you. Would you be a happier person, a better person, or a healthier person? How would it affect your relationships and how you feel about yourself?

The 4th Recognition lifts the weight of guilt and anger, and the frustration that often goes with it. Freedom from the ongoing oppression of these heavy feelings tends to leave you feeling lighter, more energetic and more optimistic about life. There is a great release of stress that you have been carrying which can even lead to better overall health. So many illnesses are related to chronic stress. (Chronic stress lowers levels of dopamine in the brain and has a negative affect on mood. Chronic stress is associated with weight gain and more.) Remove the old erroneous programming in this area, and your internal stress is greatly reduced. Many of our clients say that the 4th Recognition is the most important of all the Recognitions and that it was this one which did them the most immediate good.

The 5th Recognition

Take your life in a new direction and get what you want! Discover what is really important to you, and then program yourself to have it or be it. Program yourself for success in life. Program yourself for health. Learn about and program yourself for success in your life's calling.

When you receive the 5th Recognition, write it here for reference in both the Short Form and the Full Form as you get each version.

_____

_____

_____

_____

That is what the 5th Recognition is all about. You should have been working with the first four for about a month before you receive this one. By then you will have made a great amount of headway in removing the old programming. This Recognition provides a way to plant seeds that you can now grow in that fertile subconscious mind of yours.

Good, positive things have probably already started to happen in your life by the time you get to this Recognition. We carry within ourselves all the essential, positive programs that we need to be successful. But somewhere along the way, when we were young, we picked up negative suggestions from parents, siblings, teachers and other authority figures in our lives. These negative, erroneous and even unhealthy suggestions inhibit our ability to respond to our *innate or genetic* programming. This leaves us feeling frustrated, afraid and depressed. Using the first four Recognitions removes the old erroneous programming and allows our good, positive, and natural programming for success to work for us.

In the 5th Recognition, we are able to take this a step further; not only can the original programming (probably genetic and spiritual) begin to work, but we can either reinforce it or add new programs (i.e., for business, sports, etc.).

Enjoy using this important recognition. After you have used this one for a week or so in the Short Form, you will have a much better idea of what you really want. Then go back and talk to your therapist or 7th Path™ Teacher about the Full Form of the Recognition. The Full form of this Recognition is designed to help you make specific changes in your life which are really important to you.

When you learn the 5th Recognition in the Full Form, you will be using some of the most powerful techniques and processes available to the human nervous system. You will go far beyond conventional techniques such as visualization and most forms of hypnotic suggestion.

How to construct and use your 5th Recognition in the Full Form

After you have spent sufficient time with the 5th Recognition in the Short Form, you may wish to work on specific changes. The 5th Recognition in the Full Form is taught by your 7th Path™

Teacher, and she can answer your questions or fill in any details which are not covered here.

First off, let me answer a question that I get all the time, "How long should I give myself suggestions for a specific change that I want to make before I begin working on another?" Sometimes I get asked, "How many different changes should I or can I work on at one time?" When it comes to giving yourself suggestions for a specific change that you want to make such as being more patient, getting more exercise, or smoking cessation, and so on, you need to do some prioritizing. What I mean is that you need to decide which change is most important to you and then focus on that one change until it has been achieved.

Once you get that one change accomplished, or well underway, then move on to the next thing. If you start off by giving yourself suggestions for two, three or four different things, you tend to dilute the process and get nowhere on any of them. Focus on the one thing that is most important and stick with that one thing until you achieve success.

As I write this, I'm thinking of an example that I give in class. Some of the readers of this book are old enough to have seen the Ed Sullivan show on television back in the black and white days. I remember one of my favorite guests on his show; others must have liked him too because he was on several times. He was the guy who would spin plates on the end of sticks and would have a board anchored to the stage which was about 10 feet long. It was placed flat on the stage floor and had holes drilled in it about a foot and a half apart. He would then take a doweling rod (a round tubular stick) and place one end into the hole in the board that was fixed to the stage. Then he would put a plate on top of that long stick (about 6 feet long) and start spinning that plate. He would give the plate a flick with his hand to get it going and then grab the stick around its middle point and give it a spin. In a few seconds, he would have that plate just a spinning on top of that stick. He would work just on that one plate until it was quite able to spin there on its own. Then he would go on to the next one and the next one until he had about 8 of those plates just a spinning on their own. Everyone loved him. Now if one plate started to get wobbly, before he would focus on the next plate and get it spinning he would go back to the wobbly plate and give it a few more spins.

That is how I recommend you work with the changes you want to make using the 5th Recognition. Just work on one change until you really have that one thing going well for you. Then move on to the next thing that you want to work on. When that part of your life is going well for you, and if you have something else that you want to work on, go ahead and start giving yourself suggestions for that one as well. If something that you have worked on in the past starts to get a bit wobbly, then you can go back to it and reinforce it just like the plate-spinner on the Ed Sullivan Show did. Sometimes it is just like that juggling act. Maybe that is why juggling acts are always so popular at the circus or where ever; we realize that is what we do with our lives. We constantly juggle things, first working with one thing, then another until we have everything working the way we want, and then we add something else.

So, as you begin using the 5th Recognition in the Full Form, pick one thing that means a lot to you and just work on that one thing until you have it going the way you want.

Here are some simple rules to follow that will help you to develop suggestions that are really powerful. The suggestions should be short and simple. They should deal with just one issue or behavior; like I said, working with more than one issue or behavior tends to dilute the effectiveness of the suggestion.

It should be in present tense. Don't use "I will" in your hypnotic suggestion, as that is future tense. Construct your suggestions as if they were true now.

Write out your suggestions in positive terms only. Don't use "don't", never use "never, and it is best not to use "not" or "non," or any of those kinds of terms. The reason is that it can backfire on you. For example, right now I would like you to stop thinking about purple beetles! Don't think of purple beetles! Never think of purple beetles again! It is best if you do not think of purple beetles! Be a non-purple-beetle-thinker! My suggestion to you just backfired. You may never have thought about purple beetles before, but as soon as I suggest that you stop thinking about them, you start thinking about them.

When you are constructing positive suggestions, focus on what you want. Focusing and stating what you don't want is the error that so many make. They focus on what they don't want when they think that they are suggesting what they do want. For example, if you construct a suggestion for not procrastinating, it reinforces procrastination. To further this example, the following would be a very bad suggestion, "I no longer procrastinate." If you construct a suggestion for not snacking, it reinforces snacking. Here is an example of a similar bad suggestion, "I never snack between meals." Instead, ask yourself, why do I want to stop doing these things or what would I rather be doing? Use that information to construct a positive suggestion. That suggestion is then added to Delta 5 to construct the long form. Here are some extensions that you can use for Delta 5 in the Full Form. This probably won't make total sense until you have received that Recognition, but you won't need to understand this until then.

In this example, I will simply use "Delta 5" which would be replaced by the actual Recognition when you construct the suggestion:

Delta 5 … I only put good healthy things into my body (rather than, I am a nonsmoker).

Delta 5… I exercise every morning for 20 minutes (rather than, I will stop procrastinating).

Delta 5… I eat only at the kitchen table (rather than, not snack while watching television).

Delta 5… I am patient with my children (rather than, not yell at my children any more).

Delta 5… I am always calm and relaxed while taking exams (rather than, not feel nervous).

Delta 5… I always concentrate in school (rather than, I will not daydream in school).

Delta 5… I always remain calm while driving in traffic (rather than, I will stop getting so angry).

Delta 5… I consistently improve my ability to recall names (rather than, I am going to stop forgetting names).

Delta 5… I get to work every day on time (rather than, I'm going to stop being late to work).

Delta 5… I am creative and finish my book (rather than, I'll stop procrastinating).

Delta 5… I am more friendly and outgoing (rather than, I am not shy around people).

Delta 5… I am focused at work (rather than, I am not easily distracted).

Delta 5… I complete my projects (rather than, I don't go from one project to another).

Delta 5… I take time for me (rather than, I stop giving away my time to others).

Delta 5… I remember that I am responsible for how I feel and what I think (rather than, I will stop letting others get me so upset).

Delta 5… I express my talent for playing guitar (rather than, I won't avoid playing for others).

Delta 5… I am a great golfer (rather than, I will stop getting the yips).

Delta 5… I am a terrific public speaker (rather than, I will stop stuttering).

Delta 5… I am the best salesperson where I work (rather than, I will stop making excuses).

Delta 5… I am a great _____. (You get the idea.)

Then, we take things to an even greater level of effectiveness. You may have heard about visualization. Visualization techniques are impotent compared to what you will learn as you find out how to fully use the 5th Recognition.

The 5th Recognition is different from all of the Recognitions that came before it. The others were mainly about emptying the cup; this one gives you the power to fill the cup. The essential part of the cup-emptying Recognitions was the Echo. This Recognition, when used to fill the cup, does not include the use of an Echo. We will do something much more powerful. First, you make your Delta 5 suggestion (e.g., Delta 5… I am a terrific public speaker.) Then you go directly into a process consisting of two fantasies.

Fantasies are different from mere visualization. In visualization, you are expected to see yourself doing something as if you were looking at a movie. This is a very difficult thing to do for many people. It is also very artificial. We come pre-wired, meaning genetically programmed, to do something that is more effective. That thing is fantasy. Fantasy does not involve imagining yourself on a screen. It is the process of pretending that you are *in* a situation.

It is also more than mere visualization because visualization means seeing by definition. Fantasy includes all of the senses. A good fantasy involves the six senses! That is right, I said six senses. Here they are: see, hear, taste, touch, smell, and feel (or it could be called the physical experience of emotion). That is right, the often-ignored sixth sense: the ability to feel emotionally. Such feelings involved in a good fantasy are love, joy, euphoria, excitement, sexual arousal, satisfaction, confidence, security, and many more.

Another problem with mere visualization is that it can be quite a laborious or even painful experience. Fantasies are always pleasurable! They are fun to do! Since fantasies are fun and enjoyable, you will tend to want to do them. They become something that you will look forward to doing.

Let me give you an example of the power of fantasy and how it is natural to all human beings. For most adolescent boys and girls, the idea of being completely naked with someone of the opposite sex is a scary idea. Nature had to come up with a way to overcome this or the human race would very quickly die out. Nature overcame this fear of being naked by giving us a process that we call fantasy. It works like clockwork. When the hormones hit, despite all of the insecurity that we experience at that time in our lives, we will begin to fantasize being in sexual relationships. The fantasies are both sexually arousing and pleasurable. It is through this process that we learn to associate a great deal of pleasure in being naked with someone of the opposite sex. Due to the success of this process, it looks like the human race will continue for a long time.

Back when we were indulging in adolescent or teenage fantasies, we were *not* seeing ourselves on some kind of movie screen; we imagined that we were with our fantasy lover. We "pretended" that we were with him or her. We were able to use all of our senses. If we wanted, we could hallucinagentically fantasize the feeling of touching his or her skin and hair. We could also taste and smell the scents associated with being in that situation if we want to, and we could certainly feel the passion grow inside of us, given such a fantasy. We still have those fantastic fantasizing abilities today.

This is why I promote fantasy. It works. It is natural. We have already practiced it and are probably already pretty good at it.

We use two kinds of fantasies when doing the 5th Recognition. First you will do the "fantasy of doing it", then the "fantasy of receiving it".

The process of self-programming using the Full 5th Recognition goes like this:

1. Say the first five words of Delta 5.

2. Follow that with the suggestion.

3. Experience the fantasy of doing what needs to be done to accomplish what you want.

4. Experience the fantasy of receiving the rewards of accomplishing the goals associated with the suggestion.

The "fantasy of doing it" requires some explanation. With the fantasy of doing it, you need to remember that this *is* a fantasy. That means you get to imagine that you are doing what you fantasized in an enjoyable way. For example, let's say that you want to ride your bicycle every morning for 20 minutes. One of the reasons that you don't already do that is because you imagine how difficult or painful that might be. In a fantasy of doing it, you have the fantasy of doing it like you had already been doing it for years! Fantasize that you are on that bike and it is easy and fun. Fantasize that you can easily keep up a good pace. There are no limits to fantasy. Fantasize that you are winning a race!

The fantasy of doing attaches an expectation of pleasure to the process you want to do. This kind of programming is very powerful, but the next fantasy really seals the deal.

The "fantasy of receiving it" is simply the fantasy of receiving all of the benefits that you would expect from completely achieving the goal associated with the suggestion. In the example above, the reason for riding the bike every day for 20 minutes may be that you want to lose some weight or firm up. Maybe you want to have a healthier heart. So, in the fantasy of receiving it, you simply move to experiencing the goal. For example, you may have a wonderful fantasy of yourself on the beach looking great! There you are looking so great that you make mouths fall open as you walk by (after all, it is a fantasy!). Or, you could have the fantasy of being with your doctor at a physical examination a couple of months down the road (that is a bicycle pun) and he or she is stunned with how well your heart is pounding away, like someone half your age!

Warning! I did this same exact thing back when I was just getting into bicycling. By the time the snow fell (I was living in Minnesota back then), I was routinely putting in 18 to 25 miles on my bicycle nearly every morning before I came into work, and even more miles on the weekends! This is very powerful stuff!

The 5th Recognition can be used as a Solution Generator!

The state of hypnosis gives you access to more brain power than when you are in the normal waking state. In hypnosis, you are able to access vast amounts of subconsciously held bits of information. With the proper instructions, this information can be used to generate solutions to many challenges in your life. In 7th Path™, the instructions are given as suggestions to yourself while doing the 5th Recognition.

To use this fantastic solution generator, here is all you have to do: When doing the 5th Recognition, just add this statement to the short version of the Recognition (after the first four words, "How can I _____.") Then fill in the description of the solution you want.

Here are some examples:
- How can I exercise every day and enjoy it?
- How can I remember to do my 7th Path™ every afternoon and make it automatic?
- How can I get to work on time every day and make it fun?
- How can I help my children remember to do their homework and enjoy it more?
- How can I always be more patient with my family?
- How can I make my visits to _____ more pleasant?

Notice that the solution is described exactly as you want it. I suggest that you end each description with something that makes the solution enjoyable or pleasant. Would you want your brain to generate solutions you would find pleasant or enjoyable? I would, and that is why I like to construct my suggestions with endings such as, "and make it fun to do."

Useful variations on this approach consist of changing the "How" questions into "who," "what," "when," and "where" type questions. I don't recommend "why" questions because "why" instructs your mind to focus on the problem rather than the solution. If you were to ask, "Why don't I exercise every day" your mind may become an excuse generator! It will come back with things like, "Because you are too tired," or "Because you are too lazy!"

When you use the Solution Generator, I suggest that you stay with a particular question for a while. The longer you stay with the process, the more creative the solutions will be. Often, when you are first working on a solution in this way, you will get some of the answers that you could have come up with without using this approach; however, after some time, you will be surprised at the new solutions that will be generated.

Now construct some of your own suggestions and show them to your 7th Path™ Teacher if you want to. (No, you don't have to share your fantasies with anyone if you don't want to.)

_____

_____

Chapter 10
The Advanced Recognitions

I am going to only briefly discuss the next four Recognitions at this time. Your hypnotherapist or 7th Path™ Teacher will be happy to go over them in more detail as you receive each one. For the most part, the first five Recognitions are just the beginning! I recommend that you do the work of the first five Recognitions, and then get the Advanced Recognitions. They are simply transformational. If you like, you can use the goal of getting these Advanced Recognitions to help you to discipline yourself to do your Basic Recognitions each day in preparation for these wonderful advanced vibrations.

Using the 6th through 9th Recognitions tends to work best if you are able to conceptualize some level of spirituality in your life. However, that being said, I do think that if an atheist really wanted to use the Advanced Recognitions, she could do so and benefit greatly from them. It would just take a greater level of creativity in coming up with Delta words that did not imply some kind of spirituality. It would be perfectly okay if such a person would like to receive those Recognitions, if the motivation is really there to receive and use them.

Having said all of that, now let me say that receiving and using these Advanced Recognitions can be some of the most moving and inspirational spiritual experiences that you have ever hoped for. So many times, when giving these Recognitions to my students and clients, they were met with tears of gratitude and feelings of awe!

When will you be ready to receive the Advanced Recognitions? To truly experience fullness of these Recognitions, the practitioner must have put in sufficient time with the Basic Recognitions, to what I call, "prepare the vessel." As a guide, I recommend that you spend at least one week on each of the Short Forms and one week on each of the Recognitions done in the Full Form. This means that the dedicated 7th Path Self-Hypnosis® Practitioner can be ready for the Advanced Recognitions in about ten weeks.

So many times, I am asked, "What is it like to do 7th Path Self-Hypnosis®?" or "What will I experience?" Everyone's experience is somewhat different, but by observing the experiences of so many students, I can tell you what it tends to be like for most. Only through experiencing each Recognition and having your own valid experience can you know what it will be like for you. This is an *experiential* teaching. With that in mind, I will proceed and let you know more about what each of the Advanced Recognitions are about, and what tends to be experienced by practitioners who have told me their personal experiences with using them.

The 6th Recognition

The 6th Recognition is the doorway to the Advanced Recognitions. It provides you the insight to enter into a partnership with your Delta. This Recognition brings you to a level of understanding that you are in a relationship with your Higher Power and that you are never alone in doing what you came into this world to do.

When you receive the 6th Recognition, write it here for reference in both the Short Form and the Full Form as you get each version.

_____

_____

_____

_____

When you receive the Short Form of this Recognition, you begin to *experience* a level of responsibility in this relationship. Reinforcing this awareness can really cause a powerful shift in your realization about how you create your life. This is a truly awe-inspiring Recognition.

Using this Recognition empowers you like none of the others. It opens up a conduit for the Delta Energy to begin to flow towards you like never before. It was always there, but now you have a way to access it, to realize it and to begin to live it fully.

Receiving and using this Recognition in the Full Form provides you with the understanding you need to maximize your confidence in doing whatever you came into this life to do. These Advanced Recognitions take advantage of the fact that you have made significant gains in removing the old programming that has held you back for so long. Now you can move forward in a kind of partnership that you have always had, but somehow had forgotten. With this understanding, you begin to vibrate at a higher level, and that energy is experienced with a new found confidence and understanding regarding your place in the world.

When you go from the Short Form to the Full Form of the 6th Recognition, you understand even more profoundly that this partnership has always existed no matter what you were doing in your life. Perhaps you will even begin to sense that Delta has always been working toward the one goal of assisting you in doing what you came into this life to do, whatever that thing is (or whatever those things are).

Receiving and using these Advanced Recognitions (once a significant amount of the "baggage" has been removed by the Basic Recognitions) can open up a whole world of opportunity to you that was always there, but have been overlooked in the past. Whether you are not sure if you want to receive the Advanced Recognitions, or if you feel that you are not ready to receive them, I recommend that you go ahead and get this one and find out for yourself if you are ready to take this next big step. I believe that you will be very happy that you did.

The 7th Recognition

The 7th Recognition suggests that you have a purpose in life that you are fulfilling whether or not you are consciously aware of it. So many people lack the feeling of real purpose in life: "Why am I here?" "What is life all about?" "How do my actions affect others?" "Am I supposed to learn something in this life?" "Should I care?"

When you receive the 7th Recognition, write it here for reference in both the Short Form and the Full Form as you get each version.

_____

_____

_____

_____

The 7th Recognition suggests that there may be some answers to these questions. These later Recognitions will really make you think, and may change how you think of yourself in relation to others. This Recognition provides a new kind of clarity about your role in this life and in your world.

As you receive and then use this Recognition in the Short Form, your relationship with yourself and others begins to change. Your role in life becomes much, much bigger, as you realize the importance that your life has in this world (every waking minute of it). You realize that what you are thinking and doing radiates out to others, first affecting you, then those closest to you, and then outward from there.

As you use this Recognition think about those gifts which were given to you. Think about how you are like Delta. You realize that you have the opportunity to do the work that you were created to do when you make every decision or take any action during your day.

As you learn this Recognition in the Full Form, everything expands infinitely as this Recognition brings about a kind of mindfulness that makes every day so much more meaningful on the highest levels you can imagine. Your relationship with others expands, and your thoughts and actions become more meaningful.

Enjoy this new level of love, creativity and responsibility in your life. As you do that, you are enlightened, those around you are lifted and the whole world benefits.

The 8th Recognition

The Eight Recognition provides an even higher perspective on life. What is really real? This Recognition is designed to help you see *all of life* as a spiritual existence. What if both the pleasurable and the painful events in life were sacred, a gift, a blessing? What if you could see the spiritual aspect in the pain that you have experienced? Are you ready for that? This Recognition is designed to positively change your relationship with the whole world and all that is in it.

When you receive the 8th Recognition, write it here for reference in both the Short Form and the Full Form as you get each version.

_____

_____

_____

_____

Using this Recognition leads to experiencing more peace and patience in your life. This Recognition contains spiritual wisdom far beyond what most people have attained in their lives. Using this Recognition brings this wisdom into your life every day.

In the Short Form of the Recognition, you are really stretched! The logical conscious mind and the more emotional subconscious mind are set to work things out. All of creation looks different as if the light was turned on. "Oh my," you might think to yourself, "dare I think a thought so great?" Dare I let go of all that misconception that I have carried around with me all my life? Can I really start to see this level of Oneness in the world, in every thing? Receive and use this 8th Recognition, and you will find out. Once you have done this work, it all starts to connect at a level you thought was only available to the saints and the avatars!

Receive and use the Full Form of the 8th Recognition and a feeling of compassion and fullness wells up in you. You may even think, "Oh my, I can feel the truth in this one, just two more words were added and it is so much more powerful in the Full Form!" On one level you may think, "It is so easy now that I know this," and on another level you may feel its difficulty as you feel stretched mentally, emotionally and spiritually to take in this whole new way of looking at all that is. Such a sublime stretching of your consciousness! Receive and use this Recognition, and your ability to connect with others at such a spiritual level will surprise you. Most would think that they would never be able to manage this level of spiritual connection in just one lifetime. Perhaps some of you have reached this level already, and for you it will be like coming home.

The 9th Recognition

The 9th Recognition is for experiencing a direct connection to the Source, to Delta. This Recognition has the purpose of helping you increase your awareness of your connection to your creator, whoever or whatever you perceive that creative source to be.

When you receive the 9th Recognition, write it here for reference in both the Short Form and the Full Form as you get each version.

_____

_____

_____

_____

This 9th Recognition completes the process of the 7th Path Self-Hypnosis® Recognitions. It continues to assist you in seeing your whole life from a higher perspective and purpose. It helps the practitioner shift from conditional gratitude towards Delta, to a state of constant and unwavering gratitude. This Recognition also magnifies the work done in the 4th Recognition, setting you free from painful feelings and limiting beliefs regarding your past.

As you receive the 9th Recognition in the Short Form and apply it directly to Delta, a greater sense of connection to the source is established. I have seen so many tears of gratitude flow when a student receives this Recognition for the first time. It is truly a wonderful experience to have for one's self or to view from the teacher's point of view. It transforms everything that you have ever experienced in your life from whatever you have thought up to now, into what it will be from this point forward: a much greater a gift and a blessing.

When you receive the Full Form, you move up so much further. It has been described as "a quantum leap forward in consciousness." It is just two more words, but those two words transform everything that you will ever experience into something that is so much more wonderful than it would have been otherwise.

How will it be exactly for you? I cannot tell you. I can only relate to you what it has been like for me and the others who have shared their experiences with me. So many of these Recognitions contain concepts that you have thought before, or principles that you have read about, or seemingly come up with on your own, but somehow the effect is so much greater when you sit down, beginning each and everyday this way, doing the Recognitions as written.

It is truly an experiential teaching that will be different for everyone depending on so many factors, of which the most important is your interaction with your Delta. Remember, that as you do this it is always done with Delta, and the experience you have is guided by Delta, and so I know that it is perfect.

The Full Forms of the Recognitions

A quick comment about using the Full Forms of the Recognitions. They are recommended if you would like to intensify, and thus speed up, the process. Ultimately you should strive to receive all of the Recognitions first in the Short Forms and then in the Full Forms. The Full Forms help to ensure that the insights are being applied to areas in your life that might be resisting their application or where you might not have thought that they applied.

Generally, they cause a more holistic affect of the Recognitions to your life. Without the Full Forms, some practitioners may experience a tendency to receive only a partial benefit. This is because there is a tendency to apply the Short Forms of the Recognitions to only the issue that they came in to work on. The Full Forms of the Recognitions helps overcome this and provide the greatest benefit to the practitioner.

Often, the Full Forms of the Recognitions take you deeper into buried misconceptions or feelings related to long forgotten but important events from your life. Because of this, using the Full Forms can provide a more complete release of harmful beliefs and feelings. This leads to a more complete "emptying of the cup."

Ultimate Recognitions

These Ultimate Recognitions are not for the atheist! These versions of the Recognitions were designed to take you into a much more personal experience with your Delta. You need to have practiced the other Recognitions for at least a couple of months and have the desire to use this practice in a spiritual way in order to receive these Ultimate Recognitions. Using 7th Path Self-Hypnosis® you first emptied the cup, then you filled the cup, and now with the Ultimate Recognitions, your cup will overflow.

The Ultimate Recognitions really stretch your consciousness beyond anything that has come before in this practice. They work with the same kind of issues that are covered in the previous Recognitions, but they are stated in an even higher form. The ability to use these Ultimate Recognitions powerfully magnifies the work done in the earlier Recognitions. Are you ready for that?

If you are only beginning your journey on The Path, then you probably are not ready for these Ultimate Recognitions. But after some practice, you may be ready for more. When and if that happens, ask and you may receive these valuable and powerful Recognitions.

When you are ready for more, we have so much more to offer you!

Chapter 11
The Secret Language of Feelings

One of the major philosophies of the 7th Path Self-Hypnosis® and 5-PATH® Hypnotherapy is that all feelings are good when they are being generated by accurate perceptions. They are there to help guide you. All of your feelings flow from your perceptions and understandings regarding your experiences and beliefs. When you feel "bad," meaning being in some kind of emotional pain, it is a signal from your subconscious or unconscious mind that you are not fulfilling some human need, want or desire. For example, if you are feeling lonely, then you are not satisfying your need for human companionship. The painful experience of loneliness is good once its "secret language" has been understood. All emotional pain is there to motivate you to do something. Once you understand the Secret Language of Feelings, you can use the information to help you to take action. This will lead to doing the things you need to do to take good care of yourself and the people that you care about.

Problems come up when we try to ignore these feelings by stuffing them down, or by swallowing them back, or otherwise trying to deny our feelings. This kind of dissociation from our emotions leads to internal stress. Learn what your feelings mean and they will give you direction in your life. Attempting to deny your emotions and the feelings that are generated by them leads to many of the problems that we develop in life, ranging from addictions of every kind (e.g., alcohol and drug abuse, overeating, and obsessions of almost any variety) to psychosomatic illness (e.g., ulcers, headaches, bowel problems and much more).

Using both the 7th Path Self-Hypnosis® system and The Secret Language of Feelings book together is a powerful way to free yourself from addictions, self-defeating or harmful habits, and at the same time provide new insight and direction in your life.

Here are some examples that will help you begin to understand the secret language of feelings:

The feeling of anger is trying to tell you that you have perceived a situation as being unfair to you or to someone you care about. You need to seek fairness if the situation is truly unfair or forgive it if it was in the past.

The feeling of guilt is trying to tell you that you think that you have done someone wrong. You need to try and make it up to them, to make things right again, or if it was long ago and making things right is not an option then you need to forgive yourself.

The feeling of fear is trying to tell you that you are thinking that something bad might happen. You need to do a reality check. If you do a reality check and there is nothing to be afraid of, your fear will begin to leave you. If there is something bad that might really happen, then you better get busy and try to prepare for it! Fear is there to motivate you to provide safety and security for yourself and others. This is why even fear is good. (If after doing the reality check, you have found that there is nothing to be afraid of, but you still feel afraid, then it is a program running inside of you that 7th Path Self-Hypnosis® will work on. You can also have great success in overcoming this irrational fear by working with a 5-PATH® Hypnotherapist.)

The feeling of sadness is telling you that you have lost something or someone important to you. You need to try to either get it (or him or her) back or replace it (or him or her).

The feeling of frustration is letting you know that what you are doing is not working. You need to try something else. Usually frustration is a call for creativity, collaboration or expert guidance.

The feeling of being bored is telling you that what you are doing is not challenging enough for you. You need to spice up your life by adding things that are fun, interesting, or growth experiences. Maybe you need to move your body. Listen to this feeling and it will motivate you to begin living up to your potential.

With this information you can respond to your feelings in a much more satisfying way than ever before. Here is a quick explanation of how you can do that.

Take for example an individual who wants to lose weight and become healthier. This individual has a history of eating more than her body needs, and the rest is stored as fat. At the Banyan Hypnosis Center for Training and Services, Inc., we have worked with many such people. What we have found is that these people are responding to cues that have nothing to do with physical hunger. Among other things, these individuals have learned to respond to emotions with the behavior of eating.

This is such a big problem because eating does not satisfy you when you are feeling bad. It does not satisfy you because it does nothing about the cause of the feeling "bad". It only provides a momentary distraction from the emotion. When the overeating episode is done, the feeling continues to be generated by whatever is causing the emotional pain. *This is because eating cannot have any effect on the cause of painful feelings*. Eating only distracts you from the emotional discomfort that you are experiencing.

So, if loneliness is caused by not being with the ones you care about, or not having someone to love or care about, how much do you need to eat until you have someone to love? The question does not make any sense! This is because eating because of loneliness does not make any sense, but there are millions out there who do that every day. They also eat too much (or drink too much, or gamble too much and so on) because of anger, guilt, frustration, sadness, depression and just about every unpleasant experience that you can describe. They also distract by shopping, working, and using drugs, among other things.

Continuing the example of the person who is eating in response to her emotions; what she needs to do is make a simple change, and as a result, she can experience a great deal of success right away. I would simply ask her to stop and check to find out if she is hungry before she eats (and I would like to reinforce that with hypnosis).

If she is hungry, then she is to eat. If she is not, then she needs to do the following:

- Notice what she is feeling and name it.

- Notice what is happening that is causing her to feel that way.

- Respond to the feeling in such a way that it removes or changes the condition that is causing her to feel that way. I call this a satisfying response.

Here is how we can apply this to a particular feeling or emotion. Let's say that our hypothetical overeater takes my advice when she notices that she is thinking about eating something. It is not meal time. If she eats between her planned meals, it is called snacking. This would be a snack that she does not need because it will stop, or at least slow down her progress toward her goal of becoming slim and healthy. Snacking now would be a problem for her because she wants to lose weight in order to look and feel great for an upcoming special event, such as a wedding, vacation cruise, or anniversary.

First, she checks to find out if she is really physically hungry. During our time together, I showed her where that feeling occurs in her body. It is a discomfort that occurs behind the solar plexus, not in her gut. Gut discomfort has nothing to do with physical hunger, and is more likely to be an emotional response than anything else. If she is really physically hungry, then she is to satisfy that physical hunger and eat until she has eaten in a way that is healthy for her (which for most of us is surprisingly little).

If she is not physically hungry, she is to ask herself what she is really feeling emotionally. In this example, let's assume that she is feeling bored. Here is how she can respond to this feeling in a satisfying way, using The Secret Language of Feelings:

- She identifies the feeling as being bored.

- She realizes that the feeling is being generated by the condition of being in a state of insufficient challenge or growth. This is caused because she was sitting around watching reruns on the television and they are reruns of programs she would not have even watched the first time around! She's just filling up time with mindless junk.

- She listens to what the feeling was telling her to do and she begins to engage herself in things that are more fun, interesting, etc. For example, she might:

- Call a friend.

- Read an interesting book.

- Get on the Internet and do some research.

- Go for a walk.

- Study something of interest to her, and so on.

- Write in some of your own ideas here. _____

- _____

- _____

When it comes to the feeling of being bored, one thing that we know for sure is that just about anything she puts on this list is going to be infinitely more satisfying than anything she can eat. Eating does not satisfy the underlying cause of being bored (that of being unchallenged); eating is just not that much of a challenge even though it can be very enjoyable. It is just a distraction and distractions don't satisfy anything.

If you want to learn more about The Secret Language of Feelings, you may ask your 7th Path™ Teacher or hypnotist. Also, you can order it through our website, *www.TheSecretLanguageOfFeelings.com* or by calling us at our office, (469) 969-2176 or Toll free at (800) 965-3390.

Chapter 12
Frequently Asked Questions

This section answers some of the questions that we most often receive. When you read them you will find that your experiences are in common with other practitioners' experiences. If your question is not covered here, feel free to contact the person who provided you with this book, your 7th Path™ Teacher, or 5-PATH® Hypnotherapist.

Sometimes I can't relax. Am I doing something wrong? Probably not. Uncomfortable feelings like your inability to relax are often part of the practice. Keep going. Remember that relaxation is not required.

I used to see all kinds of colors with my eyes closed while I practiced, but I don't any more. Am I doing something wrong? Seeing colors is commonly reported but is only a side effect of the process. Be glad that you have passed through that initial phase. If they return, enjoy them. But they are not really all that important, nor are any other pictures or symbols along the way.

Sometimes I feel really antsy and don't want to finish my time. Am I doing something wrong? This is a very common experience and it generally means that *you are doing things right*. You are working on negative feelings and neutralizing them. It is important when you are experiencing this to continue to do the work, and keep your promise to yourself to complete the time that you have set aside for your 7th Path™ practice.

Sometimes I cry when I do this. Am I doing something wrong? Good work! You are going to feel great once you let all that go. Read the above question and answer.

Sometimes I don't feel hypnotized. Am I doing something wrong? Remember that hypnosis is not relaxation. It is a product of focused attention. *If you are saying the Recognition to yourself and then waiting for an Echo, you are doing everything right.*

I'm new to the 7th Path Self-Hypnosis® and have been practicing every day. I'm concerned because I'm feeling more emotional than usual. Even in between my 7th Path Self-Hypnosis® practice sessions I sometimes feel moody, angry or just plain terrible (people do not want to be around me sometimes). Is this normal? This happens in a small percentage of cases. You are in a process of releasing emotions, what we have been calling emptying the cup! In your case, the releasing of the emotions has not been limited to your self-hypnosis sessions. This is usually reported when a practitioner begins working with the 2nd or 3rd Recognitions. This is a temporary condition. It is best to respond to these feelings by saying the Recognitions to yourself in the form of an affirmation. This is called using the Recognitions as affirmation because we are using the Recognitions in the normal waking state (while not in hypnosis). Soon you will move on to the 4th Recognition which also helps to reduce and then remove these distressful feelings.

My dog or cat loves to sit with me when I do 7th Path. Is that okay? Everyone seems to find that their pets love to bother them when they do this. Some say that the pets are soaking up the positive energy that is being generated. I don't really know. In any case, I recommend that the pet go into the other room or train that little creature to leave you alone while you are doing 7th Path Self-Hypnosis®.

I'm having funny dreams, is that normal? Yes. Good work. Tell your therapist or 7th Path™ Teacher about them if you want to, or just let them go. The subconscious is at work. You are doing well.

I had a headache after doing 7th Path. Could that have caused it? I want to mention two things here. Trying too hard can give you a headache. Try doing the process in a more relaxed manner and that will usually take care of the problem. On the other hand, sometimes releasing stress can give you a temporary headache. Expect the headaches to pass. If the headaches continue it probably has nothing to do with the 7th Path™ process and you should see your doctor. It is probably coincidence that you started getting headaches at this time in your life. The 7th Path™ process cannot cause any kind of illness.

I'm not religious; will this still work for me? Yes. This system is complementary to most spiritual or religious beliefs, but such beliefs are not required. If this needs further explanation, talk to your therapist, 7th Path™ Teacher or spiritual counselor.

I love this. It changed my life. Can I become a Teacher or Hypnotherapist? Yes. It will require about 100 hours of training to become a 5-PATH® Hypnotherapist, and a bit less to become a 7th Path Self-Hypnosis® Teacher. Accelerated courses are available. Advanced degrees in psychology, medicine and counseling are not required.

I want to move along faster, what can I do? Good for you! We should all want to get as much out of this as possible. Here are some things that you can do:

- Commit more time to the practice.

- Keep the time that you set for each practice.

- Use the EFT Technique with 7th Path.

- Receive and use the Full Form for the Recognitions that you have.

- Get more Recognitions: all nine and the Ultimate Recognitions.

- Remember to do it at night when you go to sleep.

- Remember to do it with your eyes open as affirmations.

What do I do with the emotions that I'm feeling? Learn about The Secret Language of Feelings. Your therapist or 7th Path™ Teacher will talk to you more about this. The most important feelings are the ones that you are experiencing in the "now." Feelings about the past that tend to hurt you indicate your perceptions about the past. Take a look at them with your present knowledge. There is some very important information there.

Nothing seems to be happening. Am I doing something wrong? All good things come to those who wait and continue the process. Everyone is different, that is why you have a guide in the process. Talk with him or her to make sure that you are doing everything as taught. Something will happen. Most often when we hear this, it is because you are not waiting for the Echo and just saying the Recognition over and over again.

Do I have to do this forever? No, but you may want to.

How do I get with others that use the 7th Path? Be a good example of how the process has helped you in your life and others will want to know what you have been doing. Tell them about it and encourage them to get with your teacher so that they can learn to do it as well. Your teacher may have meetings set up where 7th Path Self-Hypnosis® Practitioners get together. If not, encourage her to do so, or if you like, arrange the meetings yourself.

I know others who are doing this and their experiences are all so different from mine. Am I doing something wrong? Everyone is different. Your experiences are perfectly valid for you when you are doing the technique correctly.

Sometimes I want to spend more time than I set aside for doing the 7th Path. Is that okay? That is perfectly okay so long as it is not interfering with other important things in your life like your job and family. Some people make a practice of doing 7th Path™ for an hour twice a day. What a luxury!

I have heard that some people spend hours at a time doing this. Is that really healthy? From time to time doing extended hours of 7th Path™ can be a really beneficial and/or enjoyable practice. But don't become so "heavenly high you are no earthly good!" (I wish I could remember where I first heard that.) Experiment with this; some people really like doing long sessions and some do not. Spending more time doing 7th Path™ tends to speed up your progress. My only concern here is that the practitioners who are spending extended hours doing this should be doing so to move them along in life, and not as a way of avoiding life.

Do I have to be a vegetarian to do this? No, just take good care of your body. There are no dietary restrictions. This is not a religion. 7th Path™ practitioners will naturally find that over time they tend to become more concerned about what they are eating. There is also a tendency to feel more motivated to exercise (just some natural programming going to work).

If all feelings are good, how come we are trying to remove them? We are only neutralizing feelings that get in the way of your success, such as anger and fear and those that are based on erroneous beliefs. You get to be the judge of whether they are built on erroneous beliefs or not. You are the one in control, you and your Delta, that is.

I'm a Christian (or Catholic, Buddhist, Muslim, etc.) and I don't want to do something against my faith. Are you sure this is okay? I have never heard of any of the Recognitions conflicting with any of the major world religions. If you are worried about one of the Recognitions, talk it over with your hypnotist or 7th Path™ Teacher, minister, or spiritual leader. You can always stop using any or all of the techniques if you feel uncomfortable with them in any way. I think that they tend to promote your spirituality whatever that is.

I've been doing this for several months and sometimes I still get angry or frustrated or feel sad. Am I doing something wrong? No. All feelings are good, even anger, frustration and sadness. As you learn the language of feelings, they will become more useful to you. What should be happening for you is that the intensity of these feelings overall will go down. You should find yourself responding with a more appropriate level of emotion to a situation that you find yourself in.

I'm having some very interesting experiences...

- Periods of absolute peace.

- Feelings of being one with All That Is.

- Feelings of compassion and love for others.

- Understanding my own religion better than before.

This is very common; consider yourself blessed. Keep up the good work and spread the word.

I have been having strange dreams, and remembering them. Is that normal? It sure is. This is reported all the time. We don't know why this happens but my educated guess is that all of the 7th Path Self-Hypnosis® that you are doing is causing a great deal of reorganization at the subconscious level of your mind, and at night that process is experienced as dreams.

My friends want to get more information about 7th Path™. Do you have a brochure or other materials I can give them? Yes, we have such materials. Give us a call, talk to your hypnotist, or 7th Path™ Teacher. We can give them to you or we can send them out for you. Our number at the Banyan Hypnosis Center for Training & Services, Inc. is (469) 969-2176 or (800) 965-3390. You and your friends can also visit our website at *www.HypnosisCenter.com* or *www.7thPathSelfHypnosis.com.*

Chapter 13
Write Down Your Recognitions

As you receive each Recognition write them below so you have one place where you can find them all. That way when you do your practice you can place this book with this page up in your lap and take a peek at them if you forget the wording of a Recognition.

For best results, we suggest that you receive a minimum of the first 5 in their Short Forms. Getting the Full Forms tends to increase the rate at which you achieve success. The Full Forms also tend to broaden the benefits in your life. Most people come to the 7th Path Self-Hypnosis® system because they are not happy with some particular area of their lives. Using the Full Forms tends to cause the benefits of the system to be applied to the other areas of your life.

Again, if you have any questions, please ask. We will be happy to answer any questions about our system.

1 **Short Form** _GOD renews my Life_
  Full Form _Mentaly phisicly, Emotionaly_

2 **Short Form** _GOD made me Always Lovable_
  Full Form _Just as I am._

3 **Short Form** _GOD Knows theres Nothing Wrong with me_
  Full Form _And there Never was._

4 **Short Form** _As GOD forgives I forgive._
  Full Form _even myself._

5 **Short Form** _GOD gave me Free will and the power to_
  Full Form _____

6 **Short Form** _____
  Full Form _____

7   Short Form _____

    Full Form_____

8   Short Form _____

    Full Form_____

9   Short Form _____

    Full Form_____